IOWA STATE
HOCKEY
AND
AL MURDOCH

IOWA STATE
HOCKEY
AND
AL MURDOCH

BUILDING A DREAM

AL MURDOCH

WITH TIM HARWOOD

THE
History
PRESS

Published by The History Press
Charleston, SC
www.historypress.com

Copyright © 2023 by Al Murdoch, with Tim Harwood
All rights reserved

Al Murdoch photograph from the author's collection. Other photographs by Bernie English.

First published 2023

Manufactured in the United States

ISBN 9781467153928

Library of Congress Control Number: 2022949638

For Jane and our five children,
who experienced many of the events in this book firsthand,
and for our nine grandchildren,
who may have heard a few of these stories before.

CONTENTS

PREFACE

"You can't go to Iowa State without going to a hockey game, and you can't make the dean's list without giving the Zamboni driver a high-five."

For years, that was something I told students in residence halls and shared with fraternities and sororities during presentations about Cyclone hockey. If you ran into me at the university between 1969 and 2021, you might have heard a few other familiar sayings. Some of them pop up as chapter titles or elsewhere in this book. A few probably shouldn't be printed. Looking back on more than fifty years in Ames has meant remembering some funny stories and some sad moments, but generally, it meant remembering a lot of great people. I did not expect to be at Iowa State—or even in the United States—for more than a few years. I couldn't have anticipated much of what happened in my story, but I wouldn't trade it either.

Before starting, let me share just a few words about what you won't find in this book. First, this is not a game-by-game or even a season-by-season account of Cyclone hockey. Like any term paper or report, this book was written within a minimum length and a maximum length, and it is much closer to the maximum.

A complete Iowa State hockey chronology would be a wonderful project for a history or sports management graduate student, and I would look forward to working with them if that person came along. However, this book is a more personal remembrance. It begins before I came to campus and includes details that sometimes stray from Hilton Coliseum and Ames/ISU Ice Arena. A vast majority of my players and teammates are *not* mentioned specifically. Whether their names appear in these pages or not, each Cyclone player is an important part of this story. I believe that—whether he played in just one game or throughout all four years. The same can be said for many others who were outside the glass but made hockey possible at Iowa State, such as cheerleaders, sales staff, pep band members, volunteers, and fans.

Secondly, this book does not analyze or propose solutions to Iowa State hockey's current challenges. I may have been referred to as "Dr. Hockey," but this is not a prescription. I was an Iowa State baseball fan; I had great respect for the national championship Cyclone men's gymnastics teams under Ed Gagnier. Those programs and several others are gone today, and I wake up in the middle of the night troubled that the same thing could happen to hockey on campus. I know many others feel the same way.

One reason for hope is that Iowa State hockey never had athletic scholarships. For NCAA teams, that is often the biggest expense and can impede a program's survival. It won't be an obstacle for the rebuilding Cyclones. If there is something in this book that can help future Iowa State teams, I believe it is the stories of determination, perseverance, and creativity (mine and others) that made us successful for the forty years I spent there as a coach and player. More of those qualities will be needed in both the short and long term.

Another of my familiar sayings was "Word of mouth is our best publicity." I hope you will find something about Iowa State hockey that interests or inspires you. Whatever it is, I also hope you'll use that story or saying when the metaphorical game is on the line in the third period and share it with your teammates, too, whoever they are.

ACKNOWLEDGEMENTS

"Hey, that's fascinating. You should write a book." No one can guess how many times that suggestion has been made to people with accomplished résumés and interesting experiences working in every imaginable career field. The fraction of times these potentially fascinating books make it onto the page is inestimably small. My children were a major reason the "you should write a book" sentiment took form as what you are reading today. They believed I should share my stories. More than that—they took definitive steps to make it happen.

Thanks are also due to The History Press. They have published thousands of titles about interesting topics from every part of the country, preserving the legacies of many communities and organizations in the process. In particular, I'd like to thank Chad Rhoad for his interest and know-how.

I am grateful for the *Iowa State Daily* student newspaper and the university yearbook, *The Bomb*. From the very beginning of hockey on campus, their coverage helped inform the entire university community about the exciting things a small group of students were doing. Today, that coverage represents a valuable record.

The book is enhanced by many photographs taken by Bernie English. When he could have been enjoying a leisurely retirement, he was working hard in many capacities for Iowa State hockey, because he believed in what we were doing. Every week of the season, he would give me a packet of pictures, which were his own way of telling our team's story. Bernie passed away in 2009 after eighty-two lively years. I am pleased we were able to honor him with a place in the ISU Hockey Hall of Fame in 2002.

Speaking of halls of fame, I am proud to be a member of five of them: the Iowa State Hockey Hall of Fame, the American Collegiate Hockey Hall of Fame, the Brandon University Sports Hall of Fame, the Bemidji State University Athletics Hall of Fame, and the Ames Minor Hockey Association Hall of Fame. While not directly related to writing this book, it is tremendously gratifying to know that each of these organizations felt I was an example of their most important ideals.

Finally, I am grateful to the Ames hockey and skating community. It was always important to have as many ice users as possible. Over the years, this helped justify to Iowa State University and the City of Ames that various facilities were worthwhile. I am pleased that youth hockey in Ames is strong and growing, and I am proud that my family and I have been part of that success.

1

MURDOCHS WILL BE THE BEST

"You don't run to finish second." That was one of the important lessons that stayed with me from my dad. I was the last born in the Murdoch family. My two brothers and my sister were all ahead of me; they had left home, and my mother was a schoolteacher, so my dad was the only one I had to talk to as a boy on the farm outside Neepawa, Manitoba. I would ask him to tell me about what it was like when he was young and some of the things that he had done. Imagining him at my age, I found those stories to be very interesting.

Alexander Murdoch—he often went by Sandy—was born in Scotland just a few days into the twentieth century in January 1900. His mother passed away when he was about a week old, but he went to live with his mother's family in the highlands until he was nine or ten years old. After so many years, they wrote to his dad to come get him because times were tight, and they couldn't afford to keep him anymore. His father had remarried in Glasgow, but for my dad, leaving his mother's family and the home he had known must have been hard.

Still, in Glasgow, he had the opportunity to do new things. He sang in church and had a wonderful voice. Of course, he was interested in any competition there was, and in Great Britain, that meant playing soccer. Someone saw how fast he was on the soccer field and said, "Hey, there's a race coming up this weekend. You better get in this race." He won it and then got invited to others, and he kept on winning. Going to different races around the country, they would have prizes, like silver spoons and silver cups, so he accumulated a certain amount of material that had value. He always ran to win.

World War I was being fought as my dad was growing up. He enlisted and trained in Scotland, but the war ended without him being called to the front in France. As a young man, running continued to be important to him (he ran middle distance—anywhere from a mile to six or eight miles). He spent two years as captain of the Scottish Harriers Running Club. One particular race stood out, because the two best finishers would win the chance to run in Paris. It was a hot summer day, and after many laps, he saw that there were two runners ahead of him. My dad knew he could catch them, so he ran even harder through the heat. He passed the second-place runner and could see the first-place runner not that far ahead, so he got past him, too. But he used up too much energy and exhausted himself, allowing two other runners to catch him before reaching the finish line. He came in third and didn't get to go to Paris.

I heard that story as a boy, but it was years later in Ames that I saw the movie *Chariots of Fire*. It was about British athletes training for the 1924 Olympics—in Paris.

Well, I got out of that darn movie theater and called him as soon as I got home. I said, "Dad, that race you told me about was for the Olympics in 1924? Don't you think it would have been better to just catch that second-place runner and finish in the top two?"

"Alan," he said, "you always run to win. You don't run to come in second."

That's how he taught me to approach everything I did. You compete to win, and you compete as hard as you can, even if you fall down from exhaustion. That has been my philosophy for life.

Not long after missing the trip to Paris, my dad left Scotland for Canada to look for work. His past athletic accomplishments proved to be unexpectedly valuable; he had a bag full of silver spoons that he traded for food on the ship. His plan was to go to Hamilton, Ontario. Back home, someone had told him they were building cars there and that it would be a good place to go. So, after he got off the ship and traded more spoons for food and a train ticket, he started heading west.

Well, I think he fell asleep on the train. When he woke up and looked out the window, he said to the man he'd befriended, "Hey, we're in Hamilton!"

He saw the "Hamilton" sign, but it was the sign for Hamilton Street in Neepawa, Manitoba.

But he said, "We're here. This is Hamilton. This is where the jobs are. Let's get off; let's get a job."

Sure enough, there was a farmer standing on an empty hay rack, saying "I need two workers."

So, my dad said, "Hey, look. He's offering us a job. My buddy and I will take it!"

They got on the hay rack and began riding, eventually starting a conversation.

"So, what kind of work will you have us do?"

"It's down the road here a couple of miles. You'll do some stooking."

Now my dad was thinking, "Maybe my buddy will know what the hell stooking is."

They eventually made it to the field, and the farmer said, "OK, here you go. I'll pick you up at dinnertime."

My dad looked at his friend and said, "OK, what's stooking?"

"I don't know. I was hoping you'd know what stooking is."

Fortunately for them, across the road was another field where sheaves of grain had been arranged to stand up together. That's what a stook is: several sheaves placed together to keep the rain from getting in the grain. Realizing this must be a stook, they took one apart and put it back together. Then they went to their field and did the whole thing before the farmer came back.

"Very good. You did a great job. You're hired."

The work my dad did was for little more than room and board, but he got to know the area farmers. Before long, he was leading a local soccer team, and on the weekends, if there was a dance, my dad would sing. He could play just about any instrument. Even without a lesson, he had a natural knack for being able to play the piano, the accordion and the violin. He was popular at these social gatherings, eventually becoming a key member of the community.

When things slowed down on the farm, the rural families hired my dad to drive a wagon and bring children to school. In the wintertime, he would drive a sleigh. My mother, Lyla, was the local teacher at Lorndale School, and he's the guy who drove the kids to the one-room schoolhouse. That's how they met.

By this time, it was the dirty 1930s. There was dust blowing everywhere and one crop failure after another, but a farmer named Tom Woods had done well with the land. Woods lent my dad the money to buy 360 acres.

The Cordova, Manitoba, soccer team, with Alexander Murdoch seated in the center of the front row. *Author's collection.*

Somehow, they survived, with mom earning a little bit from teaching and dad being willing to do any job on the farm.

There was an old farmhouse where my brothers, Bruce and Ian, and sister, Jean, spent the first eight or ten years of their lives. I was born in 1946, right at the time when my mother and father built a new house on the farm, so my older brothers and sister thought I was spoiled. All of a sudden, we had electricity. We didn't get a telephone in that house until I was in the twelfth grade.

I was like my dad and into anything associated with music. I took piano lessons for eight or ten years. I played the trombone in high school. I took dance lessons—Scottish dancing, tap dancing—for eight or nine years. I enjoyed that, along with playing sports. Every sport that was going, I remember my dad saying that whatever it was, the Murdochs were going to be the best. He had me convinced of that.

My first two years of school, my mother was my teacher. I went to a one-room schoolhouse with twenty or twenty-two students in eight grades. Looking back, I was the luckiest guy in the world, because I got to hear all the subjects and learn all about them. Unfortunately, a new teacher came to

As a boy in Neepawa, I was involved in both music and traditional Scottish dance when I wasn't studying or playing sports. *Author's collection.*

Lorndale when I was in the third grade, and when she would ask questions of a fourth or fifth grader, I'd put up my hand with the answer. She didn't realize what grade I was in for several months. You can say what you want about a one-room classroom and having one teacher, but overall, it was a good learning opportunity. You had the chance to hear about everything, and you could learn a lot by reading.

In elementary school, there were just four students my age. Two of those students weren't that sharp. But the other girl was really sharp, and she would just compete like heck to beat me. It was a tossup each quarter with Linda Sandstrom to see who was number one in the class. She got it about half of the time, and I got it the other half, but it was good, healthy competition. It was from my mother that I inherited the ability to do mathematics well. I got the skills for public speaking from my father.

Our farm was actually fifteen miles from Neepawa, the town where I went to high school. The bus stop was about two miles from our house. They would bus kids in from all around the area, so there were four hundred or five hundred students in the high school, over one hundred in each grade. That meant there was more competition, but I loved that.

Whatever sport was going on, I'd give it a shot. In the fall, I'd compete in volleyball, cross country and football. Three sports in one period, and that's what I wanted. In this day, they say "pick your sport." Well, I competed in them all—basketball, too, even though some of my buddies said, "Oh, you don't play basketball. It's a girl sport."

Hockey was probably number one in Neepawa, but our football team was pretty good. We played Canadian football, with a wider, longer field and just three downs. We'd compete against teams in the area, as well as teams in Portage la Prairie, and we'd even ride the bus into Winnipeg. Those teams were really good. Hockey was competitive, and I was with some guys who went on to play at higher levels. Ron Pilkey sat across from me in our high school classes, and he would miss the first part of the fall. He was out in British Columbia trying out for a junior team. Ron was good, but he died in a car accident when he was twenty-one or twenty-two. All the hockey guys were tough. They were smart, they were mean, and they drank a lot of beer.

Cross country and track were my best sports, just like they were for my dad. My last year of high school, I ran the mile, but it was the half mile where I was really good. I figured I was one of the best, but of course, the Winnipeg athletes dominated. They had paid coaches and extras we couldn't afford. Norm Lee was their best competitor in my event.

"The bigger they are, the harder they fall," my dad would say.

My dad had taught me so much about running. You don't have to take the lead right out of the blocks unless you want to get ahead and make the others sick trying to catch you. When running in a pack, find someone and run on their shoulder, just a little bit behind. He said that would make

Before our farm had a John Deere tractor, my dad worked the land with a team of horses. *Author's collection.*

them sick because they don't know who you are, and it frightens them that you're right there.

So, I followed that philosophy in the very last high school race I ran at the Manitoba Championships in Winnipeg. I was on Norm Lee's shoulder, and my dad had said, "You stay there around that last turn; then you just turn it on and sprint for the last 100 or 150 yards." I did it, but Norm came with me. I was pulling ahead of him and ran through the finish line, and Norm Lee fell. He hit the finish line: *PLOP*. He had fallen forward, and they declared him the winner.

That's always pissed me off to be honest—winning the race but getting second.

My dad was mad, too. "You don't fault a win," he said.

So, at my last high school meet, I got second in the half mile. I got second in the discus. I didn't win either event, but I was close. And I certainly hadn't run to finish second.

Neepawa was a farm town of about 3,500 people. If you went there today, it would look similar to the town I knew when I was in high school. In the 1960s, students in the bottom half of the high school class were going to find a job, whether they graduated from high school or not. My oldest brother, Bruce, only completed the eighth grade. Ian left school after his junior year. That didn't stop either of them. Bruce went into the logging industry in British Columbia, and Ian took a job in a bank, eventually becoming a manager.

Maybe the top 10 percent would go on to get degrees in advanced subjects. Not everyone had to go to college or university after high school. Some would go to trade school, and others would just get jobs with their family in the area. I was on the fence, and honestly, I had other things to think about in the months after I graduated. I had a pretty good summer job. You could make some money—at least spending money—doing custom baling of hay and straw, so neighbors hired me. I would literally work from six in the morning until nine at night. Every once in a while, I would take time off to go play baseball. We had a pretty good baseball team in the summertime. Plus, there were track meets around, and I would run in those.

Near the end of the summer, a lot of my friends near the top of my graduating class were already committed to schools and about to go somewhere. I wasn't. It was my mother who said, "Well, if nothing else, you can go to Brandon College and get a teaching certificate (like she had) and it'll still give you the flexibility to do a lot of other things." It was a one-year program. I couldn't have imagined at that time that I would spend most of the next twenty years pursing advanced degrees so far from home.

Near the end of all that time in school, I was in the fifth year of my PhD program at Iowa State. Doctoral committees want you to meet some pretty stringent standards. To be honest, I think they may have been somewhat scornful of the fact that I was teaching and coaching hockey, all while trying to get a PhD. It was a heavy schedule, but I had always worked ahead and loaded up academically since I was in grade school. Even so, I was approaching the limit where they wouldn't let me go any further, because I'd taken too much time to do it.

It was in April 1984 when I got word that my father had passed away. That was internally pretty crushing. Externally, I had to keep on doing my job as a professor in kinesiology and keep working on that last degree. As it turned out, the date to defend my dissertation landed just days after I came back from Canada after my dad's funeral.

I walked into that committee room, and the chairman said, "We've decided that if you need additional time due to the loss in your family, we will certainly grant that."

"No," I said, "I'm ready."

I can tell you, they didn't reduce the grilling. It took four hours to get through the thesis defense.

At the end, the chairman stood up, and I thought, "Well, they're going to tell me to go jump in the lake or take more time."

He said, "You've done very well. There are a couple of additional things you can do (I've discovered since then that a PhD committee always gives their candidate additional assignments), but in the interim, we are granting you the go-ahead to graduate in May with a PhD."

Then they came up and shook my hand. One or two of them even gave me hugs. And then they were gone.

It was just me in that damn committee room, by myself, for maybe a half hour to digest it all. But I'll tell you, my dad was there.

"You don't ever run to come in second."

"The bigger they are, the harder they fall."

All those things came back on that long morning. It's what I am and who I am.

2

I MIGHT BE IN SCHOOL HERE

Brandon, Manitoba, is not quite fifty miles southwest of Neepawa. The city was about ten times the size of my hometown, but it still had strong ties to farming. The college there was established near the beginning of the twentieth century. In the late 1960s—just a few years after I was there—it became Brandon University, as it is known today.

There were about 150 students like me, at the college for its one-year teaching degree program, and after their one year, they dispersed all over the world. Brandon also offered three- and four-year bachelors programs in mathematics and the sciences. It was a very good school.

During that year, I went out and student taught two or three different times. I would be in the classroom observing initially and then teaching secondarily. I got good reports, because I was always good at studying the next day's material. I could sound like an expert in it when I was teaching the next day. Most of the students in teacher training planned to go into elementary schools. Only a few, like me, wanted to teach high school, and even fewer planned to teach physical education or go into coaching, so I was unique to some extent.

It should be no surprise that sports were what I was thinking about when I arrived in the fall of 1964. I thought, "Well, I'll just go out and play football." I went out and there were two or three guys who eventually played for the Winnipeg Blue Bombers in the Canadian Football League, so all of a sudden, it was very competitive. The school team was called the Caps, and they had started practice before I arrived in Brandon. My equipment was basically the junk that was left, because all the other players had been issued their gear. I picked the best helmet and shoulder pads I could find, and they asked what position I played.

"Well, in high school, I was a tight end and a defensive back."

"We've got players for that," they said, "You'll have to be a lineman here," and I think they started me off as a guard.

I didn't back down from the challenge of playing a new position. I was quick, and I learned the things I needed to do for them to keep me around. It was a great experience.

Fall went by quickly. Football season wasn't over, and hockey was already starting at Brandon's Wheat City Arena. Fortunately, I didn't find the teacher training course to be too tough, so I could do the two sports simultaneously. There were only a few other players who were on both teams. Sometimes, teammates would jokingly call me "Mickey Mouse Murdoch" in the locker room, because my program didn't seem to be as rigorous as theirs. They'd ask, "Why are you taking teacher training? Why don't you take the three- or four-year degree in mathematics or chemistry or those other subjects?" But I knew there was still time in the rest of my life to do that. Teacher training gave me an opportunity to be involved in sports and help other people enjoy the beauty of sport.

It didn't take long to realize how good the players on the Brandon College hockey team were. A lot of them had junior-level experience, and some would go on and play professionally. I think the coaches were frightened that I was going to get killed out there. I had good speed and good conditioning; I could stickhandle, but they would see me going in toward the net and say, "Geez, it's just a matter a time." Sure enough, I got nailed and knocked to the ice, but I bounced right back up. It wasn't any worse than a football hit. I was fortunate that a few of the better football players also played hockey, so they kind of protected me as the year went along.

The games could be tough. One I remember was an exhibition at the University of North Dakota down in Grand Forks. Dennis Hextall was at North Dakota that year, and they won the Western Collegiate Hockey Association. Our game against them never finished. We got through two periods, and the referee said, "That's it. You guys don't want to do anything but fight."

So, that was it. We got several cases of beer and climbed back on the bus and headed back home.

The hockey team didn't necessarily get in trouble all the time, but we did most of the time, even after the season ended. With about a month left in the spring term, the rough-and-tumble Brandon College Caps went out on a Thursday night. Friday morning, I got the note: 8:00 a.m., be in the dean's office.

"Holy crap," I thought. "Now what?"

I went in and sat down, and the dean said, "Well, you're a bit unique among these other teachers we're training. But you're good."

I sat there wondering whether he knew about the events of the night before and the police being involved. I suspect he probably did, but he continued, "There's an opening for a physical education teacher and coach for basically any sports you want. I think you would be perfect. Would you mind interviewing?"

I quickly said, "Oh, I'd like to do that."

It was my first step toward The Pas, six hours away in northern Manitoba.

When I called home to tell my mother I had a chance to be a high school PE teacher in The Pas (it sounds like "the paw"), she said, "Where?"

To make her feel better, I asked if she wanted to ride along as company in the car on my first visit. She made sure I would have a good place to live with a local family. She saw the school I'd be working in and met some of the administrators. She was a great support. My dad did not go because he was farming, but when I came home, he said, "You know, it'll be hard. It'll be as hard as anything you've ever done, but you'll be good at it."

The Pas was an area with many Cree families. There was a reservation just across the Saskatchewan River, and their best students came to school in The Pas. The town is far enough north that Inuit youth attend the high school. I would say that, at the time, Native children made up one-third of the student population. The other two-thirds were students whose parents were in industry in the area, putting in electrical power, building roads and all of that. They were difficult jobs no one else wanted, because it was cold and remote up north.

Some of the students I taught did not realize it, but I was only a year or two older than them. I was pretty young, but I loved doing what I was doing. I would go in and start coaching at six or seven in the morning and stay until nine or ten at night. There were all kinds of different sports, and I thought it was the greatest thing ever. I encouraged my students to try everything: basketball, volleyball, gymnastics. If there was a sport I didn't know about, I would learn how to play it a day or two before the students.

As a young PE teacher in The Pas, Manitoba, for two years, I coached many sports, including boys' high school basketball. *Author's collection.*

I reactivated the high school's football team. We would go down to Swan River, Manitoba, and play there. We even went to Dauphin for a game. That was a big road trip, five or six hours one way. At the bus company, a lot of people got to know me.

"Where is Murdoch going now with the team?"

Still, my name didn't carry any weight right away. I remember talking to the bus company secretary once, and I said, "Yeah, tell your boss Al Murdoch needs a bus."

Soon, I got a call back: "Hello…yeah, is Elmer there?"

"Who are you wanting?"

"Elmer. Elmer Duck."

Somehow, "Al Murdoch" had run together and sounded vaguely like the name of a cartoon character.

Other schools looked down on The Pas, because we were located way up north. We showed them though. In the spring, we took a busload of athletes to the provincial track meet in Winnipeg. Twenty-three athletes from my team competed against the best in the province. I was proud of that and remember sharing my dad's words: "You didn't come here to finish second." And we did bring back some medals.

Outside of school, life in The Pas was totally different from life in Neepawa or Brandon. The winter days are so short, it's tough for the sun to push the temperature up at all. But winter wasn't all about being indoors. Every year, the town would have what was known as the Trappers Festival. It was held the first week of January. I don't think it got above twenty degrees below zero Fahrenheit, and there was already two or three feet of snow. So, what did the locals do? They had outdoor contests: trap setting (who could set ten traps the quickest) and flour packing (you won the flour packing contest by carrying sacks of flour from the back of one pickup truck ten yards to another pickup). Well, flour packing was the Native ladies' competition and, man alive, they'd carry up to eight hundred to one thousand pounds on their back. They could do it, and the flour was their prize. That bag of flour might have provided food for the next couple of months.

I didn't know it totally—or I ignored it at the time—but alcoholism there was present at a higher rate. I had a neighbor across the street who was a Native. The drinking got so bad for him, he took a hatchet and cut his hand off. People asked him, "Why did you do that?" Well, that was the hand that was feeding him the drink.

The local hockey team was semiprofessional or intermediate level, The Pas Huskies. They were a lot of guys with a lot of ability. I played with them for the two years I was there. Goldie Goldstrand was the coach; he was from Sweden, and the Swedes had a reputation for innovative coaching. I learned quite a bit from him. We had guys who would come up and down from professional teams, so that was a great experience and had a great effect on things that I would do further on down the road. Murray Anderson was one of my students, but he also played for the Huskies at the time. He went on to join the Flin Flon Bombers and was drafted by the Montreal Canadiens. Murray eventually made it to the NHL, playing for the Washington Capitals.

There was a sprinkling of players—half dozen or so—like that in The Pas. They were really looked up to as superstars. They had the chance to leave Manitoba for British Columbia. It's like going from Iowa to California. They might have tried out for a team and played away from home the whole winter season, and then they came back and tried to wrap up high school.

Watching hockey was totally different in that part of Manitoba, too. In the spring, when the Stanley Cup playoffs were going, if you wanted to see a game, only a delayed broadcast was available a day later. So, either you didn't listen to the scores and watched it the next day or you got a car with Murdoch. I would load up with a buddy and a couple of girls, and we would go down to a pub fifty miles south that had live TV. We did that in the spring. I still talk to those three friends to this day.

After two years in northern Manitoba, I felt some burnout, but there was a good chance I was going back for another winter in 1967. I also thought about going down to the big city, Winnipeg, and getting into a high school program there. It was early August, and I had finished my summer job driving a gravel truck near Neepawa. I taught ten months of the year; during the other two months off from school, I spent the time working other jobs. Martin Neville was one of my high school classmates, and I said, "Hey, Martin, we should take a road trip."

"Sure, where do you want to go?"

"I don't care. Should we go across to the states?"

"Yeah."

We got to Chicago and bought some stuff with the money we had saved from summer work. Then we got back on the road. In northern Minnesota, we drove by this campus that had a football practice going on, and I thought, "Geez, they're practicing already in August. That's unbelievable."

So, I stopped there and said, "Hey, I might be in school here this fall."

"You *might* be, but you haven't enrolled yet?"

And I thought, "Can't you just come and go to school?"

So, we went back to Neepawa. Martin went back to dentistry training at the University of Manitoba, and I thought "I *will* just go down to Bemidji State and enroll."

Bemidji was close enough to Canada that it wasn't always friendly. Sometimes, you heard people refer to Canadians as "Canucks." I never took it as a derogatory comment, but those people meant it to be derogatory. It was similar to us calling them Yanks or whatever. But I met some pretty good people, too, and like at Brandon College, I started with football.

Football had been going for two or three weeks when I arrived, and that's when I found out I was ineligible for the team. Since I had played hockey and football at Brandon College, under NAIA rules, I wasn't going to be able to play any sports at Bemidji State until January. Instead, they asked if

I would be interested in helping coach. I worked with special teams and the linemen, both offensive and defensive. With the defensive tackles and ends in particular, I taught them to fake one way and roll the other way to get the quarterback. In the beginning, I spent a lot of time with what was essentially the JV team, and I was still learning, too.

I didn't get into trouble too often, but I did during a game we played at the University of Manitoba. I called over our punter and said, "Hey, I've noticed the last two times you punted, all the pressure has come from your right. So, fake and run the other way." He got a thirty- or forty-yard gain on that next play, but I got chewed out. The athletic director from Bemidji State had seen me talking to the kicker. He came over and said, "You didn't tell him to do that, did you?"

I said, "Well, if the opportunity's there, I said, 'See what you can create from a broken play.'"

"They've got to follow a system," the director said, "so they're ready if they move to the varsity team."

Still, the coaches put more trust in me as the season went on. Bemidji gave me the foundation to become a more confident coach.

A lot of people would have looked at the eligibility thing as a problem, but it was probably the best thing that could have happened to me. I had done quite a bit of coaching, so I considered working with the Bemidji State team a great opportunity. Meanwhile, I stayed physically active. I got all the certifications I needed in swimming and lifeguarding so I could be a lifeguard parttime at the university's swimming pool. I learned how to sail and thought I'd died and gone to heaven. I learned how to ski and all of those things that you can do for next to nothing at a small college.

When January rolled around, I wanted to try out for hockey, but the team had already been selected. They were very good in those years, and I had a lot of friends on those teams but never played. What Bemidji did offer me athletically was a track and field team. Brandon College did not have track, so it was good to get back into competition, and that became the varsity-level sport I competed in for Bemidji State. There were some outstanding athletes on the team, and it allowed me to continue with the events that I think I was pretty good at, like middle distance running. I ran a lot of laps around Chet Anderson Stadium on a track that was half beside the football field and half behind the bleachers. Because of hockey and football, I had lifted weights and was probably more muscular than most runners, so I was pretty good at throwing the discus, too. I would get points in middle distance running and relays and then in throwing events.

I did my share of driving for the track team as well. Since I had been around and had taught school, the coaches said, "Murdoch, you go ahead and drive." I drove a station wagon with two or three teammates in the front seat, three in the middle seat and two or three in the back seat. They knew I was a little bit older and figured I wouldn't get them lost. But it was good. I could compete at that level.

That second semester was the spring of 1968, and back in Canada, there were various competitions leading to the Canadian Olympic trials. So, I said to myself, "I'll go, and I'll run the half mile and win it and then go to the Olympics like my dad tried to do in Scotland."

Unfortunately, I was in Bemidji, Minnesota, and didn't have my own vehicle. The bus would have taken too long. So, I hitchhiked from Bemidji State to Winnipeg. The normal drive time would have been four to five hours. I was on schedule until I got close to the Canadian border, where drivers were sensitive about picking up hitchhikers. The Vietnam War as going, and you could be arrested for aiding someone who was trying to avoid the draft.

I ended up about five miles from the border in a little town. It was around nine or ten at night and I walked into a bar that was open. I was still several hours from Winnipeg, and I said, "Anybody going to the border?"

There was one guy who'd had a few too many drinks, and he said, "Why? What are you doing?"

I said, "I'm going to the Olympic trials. I gotta get to Winnipeg."

So, he drove me up and dropped me off near the border. Sure enough, it all worked out. As soon as I got on the Canadian side and stuck out my thumb, the first car along picked me up.

I stayed at a buddy's house in Winnipeg, but by the time I got there, it was midnight or one o'clock in the morning, and the trials were starting at eight o'clock in the morning. I was sunburned and worn out from the road. Still, when my race started, I ran pretty well in the first lap. Actually, I ran really well and stayed with the pack, still doing what my father had taught me to do.

It was on the second lap that I realized, holy shit, those guys were running fast. I knew I could run it in two minutes or slightly less. I'd run a 1:51 at Bemidji, which is cooking for the half mile. But these guys were at 1:45, and they came in ahead of me. But I had made it up to the trials and given it my best shot, same as my dad.

My coursework at Bemidji was in health, physical education and recreation. I believed it would help make me a leader in that area of education and open a pathway to me becoming an administrator. Everything I was doing seemed to build nicely on what I had already done. Not long after I first arrived on campus, they found out that I had taught high school for two years. They were short on resident assistants, or RAs. RAs got free room and board for supervising a floor in the residence hall. I turned out to be pretty good at that, because I'd been a coach and could raise my voice. If someone had too much to drink, I knew what it would take to calm them down and get them in their room. I could manage people who were my peers.

In the two years I was at Bemidji State, I did enough to basically pay my own way through school. Back home, my dad was still farming a little bit, and my mother was teaching, but their incomes weren't such that they could afford thousands of dollars in tuition and expenses. I did the residence hall job and other jobs, lifeguarding, tutoring. I paid my own way and really had no debt when I finished my degree.

It helped that I completed all the courses in two years and two summers. Bemidji gave me credit for everything I had taken in Brandon. The football staff thought I would be back for a couple of more seasons, but that's not how it turned out. They were good people. They had an impact on me; I learned how to deal with higher-level athletes, so it was a good experience. Nevertheless, like I had in the late summer of 1964 and again in 1967, I was abruptly headed someplace new in mid-1969.

3

IT'S GREAT TO BE ALIVE IN SUNNY IOWA

The dense, cool Minnesota woods crept almost all the way to the shoulders of the two-lane highway as I drove south in August. I had acquired an old, beat up white Oldsmobile convertible. A trailer was hitched to the back holding everything I owned. It was my first trip to Ames, Iowa.

Little by little, the forest was broken up by more open landscape as I made my way toward the Twin Cities. The heat became more noticeable as the cover of the trees broke and mixed with late summer farm fields. It was almost a straight line from Bemidji to Minneapolis and then Iowa State. When I was south of Minneapolis, all I kept hearing about on the radio was this big concert in a field out east—Woodstock. It was like everybody in the world was there; the announcers talked about all the famous singers and all the fun they were having. I had to fight that convertible, because it wanted to turn left to go to Woodstock. It would have been radical. But I kept going to Iowa State, and what an adventure I ultimately had.

The topic of graduate school had come up during my last months at Bemidji State. The leadership of the physical education department said that if I stayed, I could finish a graduate degree in just a few years. That would have made me even more marketable, and I could have built on what I was already doing there. "You know, you've coached with the freshman football team for the last two years," they suggested. "You could continue on with that. Maybe be the head coach of that team and maybe move up when there are opportunities."

I told them graduate school would be too expensive, and they responded, "Well, there are assistantships."

They had my attention, but at the same time, I started to think bigger. If they wanted me to stay, maybe there were other places that would want me, too. I sent out four or five letters of inquiry to different colleges and universities.

It should have taken me three years to finish my bachelor's degree, but because I went to summer school in 1968 and 1969, in essence, I did it in two. I was still completing the last of my coursework into the first week of August. In the meantime, it was gratifying to receive responses of interest from other schools I had written to. The best letter that came back was from Iowa State University.

At the time, ISU had around twenty thousand students, compared to thirty-five thousand now. Bemidji State's enrollment was around four thousand or five thousand, so I considered it a big step up. At that time, I didn't necessarily use the term Division I, but I definitely understood that Iowa State was competing with some of the best athletes and teams in the nation. I was intrigued, and I thought it would be a good challenge.

I made it to Ames late in the evening after that long drive. I didn't know anyone or anything about the campus. I didn't know where to park. I saw a sign that said "parking ramp," so I left that beat up convertible and all my life's belongings in the parking ramp that first night. Fortunately, there weren't many people on campus yet, so taking up several spaces with that big car and trailer was no problem. I spent the night at the Memorial Union.

Early the next morning at the faculty gathering, I started to meet people so quickly I could hardly keep up. At that time, the physical education faculty included all the varsity coaches. Walking into the meeting, they introduced themselves without pretense.

"Hi, I'm Harold Nichols."

"OK."

"Hi, I'm Johnny Majors."

"Oh, OK. Al Murdoch."

Hell, I didn't want to admit to them that I had no idea who they were. I didn't follow national wrestling and had never heard the name Harold Nichols. Johnny Majors—I kind of knew he had something to do with football, but I thought, "What a unique group. This is good. This is very good."

It wasn't many years after that—eight or ten perhaps—that they relieved the coaches of their responsibility to be members of the faculty. From that point, they just coached. I think it was better when they were part of physical education.

On that morning and all throughout that fall and winter, I never really thought that I would end up staying at Iowa State for longer than two years. Now, here I am, just retired fifty-plus years later.

My salary up in The Pas had started around $3,000 (Canadian) for ten months. The second year, they increased the salary to somewhere around $4,000. That was a big increase—from $3,000 to $4,000—so I was pretty happy about that. Then I went on to have an assistantship at Iowa State, which pushed me up to $8,000 or $9,000. I thought, "Hey, this university coaching and teaching is a pretty good gig."

When I was a student at Brandon College, they offered a course on audiovisuals. If you're teaching in a school, you have to know how to run a projector and put together a slideshow and those things. I was pretty good at that stuff, and it helped me build a reputation at Iowa State. These skills went along with the video analysis of players, which was just beginning to become popular. When they asked what would be unique about the way I would teach volleyball or basketball, I said, "Well, not only would I teach students the skills, but I'd video them doing it," so they could see instant replay. Actually, the eventual title of my PhD dissertation was "Audio Tutorial Systems Approach to Recreational Learning."

It's one thing to do something on the field, but it's another thing to see yourself doing it and make adjustments. I spread those techniques out over ten to twelve sports. Video also provided a benefit for campus intramurals, because we could edit together film to train officials about what to watch for and how to make the right calls. Video made it possible to train referees quickly for the hundreds of games scheduled on campus. The varsity football and basketball teams even took an interest in video so they could teach players how officials are trained and what they were likely to be watching. It became an important part of my early years at Iowa State.

I was pretty involved in intramurals, which went back to my time in The Pas trying to get the students there to be active in every sport I could. I brought some of those activities south with me, and one in particular made a notable impression. Eventually, Iowa State University had the largest intramural broomball program in the nation. We had over five hundred

Running was always part of my life. In this photograph from the 1980s, I am finishing a marathon in Des Moines. *Author's collection*.

teams playing broomball. I would speak to students in the residence halls and say, "Hey, who wants to play hockey?" A few hands would go up. Then I'd say, "How many want to play a game just like hockey, but you do it in basketball shoes?" All of their hands went up. They would come out and play from eight or nine o'clock at night until three in the morning, one hour at a time. It became a big sport and helped establish my reputation for being creative.

For my own well-being, I ran a lot. It was hard to work everything in, but I would still go out and run. There's no shortage of places to run on a university campus. I became very familiar with the golf course and really all of Ames and the surrounding area. Later, that led to one of the famous traditions of Iowa State hockey: the mud run.

We never started practicing on the ice until we completed dryland training in the fall. I insisted that the last thing we needed to do to finish our training schedule was a three- to five-mile run, and I would lead. Some guys would try to stay with me, and I would look over my shoulder and give some of the trailers a chance to catch up. The mud run always ended in the Skunk River. I remember the freshman saying, "What is he doing? Why are we doing this?"

I told them, "It'll build character. There will be games and other times where you'll say 'Hey, I did the mud run, and I didn't drown.'"

Most importantly, we all did it together. I used a lot of psychology over the years in coaching, and it always came from my father. You know, "You run to win; you don't run to come second."

I would tell players during the mud run, "You will play better. We will win a tremendous number of third periods because of this experience."

I still get emails and notes in the mail, saying, "Hey, remember the mud run? Remember winning the third period in so many games?"

Everybody is going to have hurdles in life, and we talked a lot about those. I've had so many athletes over the years who became stronger people as a result. It was something that helped them make it through tough times.

One of the things I saw during my first week in Ames was Pammel Court. After World War II, Pammel Court was constructed for military veterans coming back from service who wanted to go to school. The housing was all Quonset huts, and each one looked like a grain silo cut from top to bottom and laid down on its wide side. The walls and roof were all metal. You could get one for forty or fifty dollars a month. They finally tore all of them down, but right up to the end, there were students who wanted to live there, because the rent was incredibly good.

Pammel Court was primarily for married students. I wasn't married when I arrived, but that happened soon. Noel Wrucke was from Robbinsdale, Minnesota, and we had been undergraduates together at Bemidji State. Our wedding was held that fall at a church in Minneapolis. A lot of her family was there, and most of my immediate family came. You always have a reception after the wedding, and I had always liked to hear my dad tell stories, so I said to my two brothers, "What do you think? Should we give Dad some time to talk?"

"Oh, no. Don't do that."

So, they voted me down immediately, saying we didn't have enough time. I've always wondered what he might have said.

Anyway, Noel moved to campus, and she provided good support with all the crazy stuff I was doing. Not long after our wedding, I picked up a copy of the student newspaper, the *Iowa State Daily*, and I saw this advertisement: "House for rent. Will waive rent in trade for farm work."

I called the number and I said, "What type of farm work? I was born and raised on a farm."

They had one question: "What kind of tractor did you have?"

I said, "A John Deere."

"The position is yours, and the house is yours. You just have to work a certain number of hours a week to get free rent."

So, that's where we lived the first two years, out on a farm in Roland, north of Ames. They had a couple of John Deere tractors, and it was an excellent farm. It was called the Franzen Farm, and it's still there. I would go out to till the field in the spring and in the fall after it had been harvested. You could pull a machine that would break down the corn stalks behind the tractor. I did all of that. There were many days that I'd go to work at the university at seven or eight o'clock in the morning, get home at five or six in the evening, have a bite to eat, give my wife and kids a hug and then get on the John Deere and go for three or four hours until dark.

They said, "You can go as long as you want." And I'd say, "Well I gotta go to work at seven or eight in the morning."

One of the attractive things about being a graduate assistant in that first year was, not only did I get paid, but I got season tickets for all of the Cyclone sports. I went to the football games, and I thought, "This is great." The team won only three or four games, and that was typical in those years. They played in the Big Eight against the schools that would eventually make up the Big XII, without the Texas universities. Win or lose, the atmosphere was amazing to me.

In the winter, Noel and I went to basketball games. Throughout the '60s, the basketball team had been right around .500, some years a little better and some years a little worse. At that time, Iowa State basketball was played in what was known as the Armory. It was an old building near the end of its usable life, but it would seat six thousand or eight thousand. I thought, "What the hell, I'll go watch basketball." And I couldn't believe it. My wife and I were there, and it was jam-packed. The stands were metal, and eight thousand people were stomping their feet. It was just a riot, and I said, "So, this is big time college basketball."

I also had season tickets for wrestling. All I remembered from Canada was the fake professional wrestling, but I thought, "Well, let's go to the wrestling." The Armory was sold out. The fans were into it. Then it got to a certain weight class. It got quiet in the building. They focused the lights and actually started lowering them down above the mat, and I thought, "What the hell is this?"

Dan Gable.

He would come out, and it was like a cat pursuing a mouse. Guys tried to get away, and he'd get them all. Gable had won something like ninety straight matches. The wrestling team in those years had multiple national champions, and they were the most notable team on campus. Gable was the best of them all, and even before he won in the 1972 Olympics, at Iowa State, he was a legend in his own time.

At that point, there was still Iowa State baseball. There was men's tennis and gymnastics and swimming. Women's varsity sports had not started yet (that was still a few years away). That's not to say there weren't women athletes. The women on campus were very involved in intramurals, from tennis and volleyball to six-on-six basketball. The women's field hockey team did, in fact, compete against teams from other colleges.

Being in that atmosphere, my expectations to go back to Canada to work in a high school started to fade. I started to think of Ames, Iowa, as the best place in the world. The Vietnam War was still happening. People were protesting on campuses across the nation. There were riots, and the national guard shot students at Kent State. But in Ames, there was nothing—no protesting, no shootings, nothing.

I found that people from Iowa were like people from Manitoba. Many of the people I met at Iowa State could have been from Neepawa. Admittedly, it was a little different being from anywhere else in the world, and I could relate to the international students who came from India, Pakistan and Africa. However, I had learned from my father and my mother—I think they both had an influence on me in this regard—that you treat people fairly and with respect. I think most of the people I met in Iowa felt the same way.

There were a number of other Canadians on campus, and there was one in particular who was part of the physical education faculty. As a hockey player growing up in Canada, Chris Murray had been a goaltender. His major athletic accomplishment was being part of the Canadian Olympic track team in 1964. He was a good runner—a marathoner, basically skin and bones—and had been in Ames for probably three or four years. He coached track, and when the opportunity came to start the women's running program, he had great success and several national championship teams in cross country during the 1970s.

It was Chris Murray who said, "Oh yeah, you've got to come and play hockey with us."

4

LACE 'EM UP

Iowa State students were playing hockey at least as early as the mid-1960s. When people say, "Murdoch started hockey at ISU," no, Murdoch didn't. Chris Murray was one of the original people involved as player/coach and faculty advisor. Larry Jack was a defenseman and one of a few players who had been on the team for some time. Originally from St. Paul, he was the Iowa State captain in 1969. Larry was an excellent and dedicated student. It took an exceptional effort to be conscientious about classes and also play hockey at Iowa State during that time, because there was no rink on campus.

The earliest ISU games had been held in an adult league at the Des Moines Ice Arena, and eventually, other Iowa colleges began to field teams there. The real attraction at the Des Moines Ice Arena was the Des Moines Oak Leafs team in the professional International Hockey League. I can remember going to my first Oak Leafs game, and you could not see from one side of the ice to the other because of the cigarette smoke. Ivan Prediger was the player who made the biggest impression on the fans. He was the goon, and you didn't pick on any of his teammates. If things got slow and boring, he'd pick a fight with somebody to get the crowd going. That rink on Hickman Road in Urbandale was an eighty-two-mile round trip from campus, but it became the hub for the loosely organized Iowa Collegiate Hockey League. Drake had a team, Graceland had a team and Grinnell had a team. Eventually, Dordt College in northwest Iowa had a team. Crawford Hubbell operated the rink, and he was no dummy. If he could find other programs to rent ice in the building or help sell Leafs tickets, he was willing to give it a try.

An Iowa State game at the Des Moines Ice Arena. Before Plexiglass, metal fencing separated the fans from the players. *Author's collection.*

I had my skates and gear with me when I came to Ames, but I didn't know for certain there would be an opportunity for me to play until after I arrived. Ultimately, I enjoyed the comradeship I had with players from all over North America, along with a few Canadians. Graeme Doyle was one such player, and Dave Frankling was another. Their families had worked for Massey Ferguson building farm machinery in Ontario and were transferred to a plant in Des Moines. They were instrumental in starting the original Des Moines youth hockey program.

Some early Iowa State players were actually from Iowa. Dave Lee came from the small town of Rake, only a mile or two from the Minnesota border, as far north as you can go. His family had a barn, and in the wintertime, they flooded the floor, so that's where he learned to skate. We called it Rake Ice Arena, and when we had time off from school during one Thanksgiving break, we went there to practice. There wasn't much room, but they put down natural ice when it was cold enough to freeze, and the barn walls at least blocked the wind.

With the long trip to and from Des Moines Arena, we wouldn't practice much until the weather got really cold. For a time, we practiced on the tennis courts that had iced over. Later, we were able to collect donated materials to construct an outdoor rink north of Beyer Hall on the west edge of campus. We picked that spot because Beyer Hall was a tall building and it provided shade so the ice wouldn't melt each day. With help from the fire department, we flooded the rink, and the whole thing came together in just a couple of weeks.

There was a lot of interest in this ice on campus for open skating and intramural hockey. The first thing you know, I said, "Well, we can put four-by-four posts up on each end, then string cables between these poles and hang light bulbs from them." Eventually, that caught the attention of some administrators when they were driving home in the evenings. Our no-frills practice rink didn't necessarily match the aesthetics of this campus and its beautiful buildings. As time went on, some of those administrators took to describing our outdoor ice as "Al Murdoch's Used Car Lot." I just wanted our guys to be able to practice on a regular basis, rather than only playing one or two games on a weekend with no practice. That extra ice time made a lot of difference.

Drake was our biggest rival in that era, and they also had an excellent football team at that time. They would recruit some of their football players from Canada. Of course, those Canadians had hockey experience.

(*Left to right*) Chris Murray, Roger French (standing in for his dad, Rod), me and Dave Lee, inaugural ISU Hockey Hall of Fame members. *Bernie English.*

Before ice was installed at Hilton Coliseum, an outdoor rink—"Al Murdoch's Used Car Lot"—was the only place to practice on campus. *Author's collection.*

I remember going into one of those early games thinking, "I'm from Neepawa: I can play with the best of them," stickhandling down, and scoring. One of their players did the same thing, and I told myself, "He's not going to do that again."

The next time he was down near the top of the circles in our defensive zone, I didn't even bother trying to take the puck away. I just laid him out. Then I picked up the puck and swung around the edge of the net to break it out. That's the last thing I remember. The guy I'd hit was a football player from Edmonton, Alberta. He had gotten up and knocked me cold on my feet with a crosscheck to the face. That was in the days when they didn't check out concussions too closely, so I missed the next shift, maybe. I was back out there playing, but I was pretty dizzy, and part of my face was paralyzed for about six months. When something like that happens, you know it was a pretty good hit to the head.

These Iowa Collegiate Hockey League games would sometimes start at midnight after the Oak Leafs had played. We said to ourselves, "There's got to be something we can do, because there could be students coming in here to watch our game who would watch the pro game, too." So, we convinced Crawford Hubbell to schedule us right at ten o'clock after the Oak Leafs were done, rather than renting the ice to a men's league or anyone else. And the students showed up. It helped that we had arranged to award a keg of beer to the team that had the most organized cheers and the best banners.

We didn't lose a game that winter against an Iowa college opponent. Overall, the team was 21–5–2. We wrapped up the year in March by going to a tournament hosted by the University of Colorado. Of course, Colorado was part of the Big Eight Conference at that time, and that would turn into a good rivalry. Their fans hated Iowa State because of football, and Iowa State hated Colorado for the same reason. Still, trying to save money in those days, we would often ask the other team to either sponsor rooms for us or help us with lodging in some way. In Colorado's case, they said, "We've got some open space in the residence hall." It turned out their housing policies were a little more liberal than those of other places, so we were in a coed residence hall. Try doing room checks and enforcing a curfew in those circumstances. Geez, it was a zoo. That was our first Big Eight hockey tournament. We didn't win that one, but Iowa State and Colorado played in the finals several times over the years, and we eventually won the event a few years later in 1974.

Chris Murray and I believed there was interest that could make hockey and other ice sports a big part of the Iowa State student experience. By early October 1970, we had already signed up more than 180 players for intramural hockey, and eventually, there were about twice that many who played that winter. They were ready to start as soon as it was cold enough to rebuild the outdoor rink for a new season. Chris and I could imagine skating clubs and physical education classes for credit, available to both men and women on campus. Our goal was always to make ice available to the largest possible number of students and to promote interest among as many people as we could.

There were some changes to the hockey team that fall. The biggest was that Peter Slater was brought in as head coach. Slater's older brother was the head coach and general manager for the Des Moines Oak Leafs at that time. Peter was twenty-two years old. He had been at Oberlin College in Ohio the year before, and we encouraged him to attend Iowa State and work on his master's degree. Well, it turned out he only spent half a year with us; he left school and went to play for the Oak Leafs. Eventually, he made it in the

World Hockey Association. When he left campus, it opened up the door for me to become a player/coach at midseason.

I was probably the pushy guy, and maybe that's why I became the coach. I made my teammates give a little bit more, travel a little bit further, fundraise a little bit more aggressively. Those things were all part of being on the team at that time. The membership fee was just three dollars for the 1970–71 season. Chris Murray was still the faculty advisor, and before the season started, he told the players, "You're going to have to maintain the outdoor rink. You're going to have to promote hockey. You're going to have to recruit fans and sell tickets."

At just a few dollars per player, we had to do a lot to provide the kind of first-class situation we wanted for the team. It was our goal to buy five sticks for each skater and make sure everyone had a helmet. We even hoped to raise enough money to buy our own skate sharpener. The team did have matching uniforms, and that was important. Some of the teams we played at that time did not.

The *Iowa State Daily*, the student newspaper, loved us. That helped get the campus excited about Iowa State hockey. Here we were, a bunch of bumpkins who weren't on scholarships. We were playing for the fun and joy of playing. We did not have a huge budget, but we performed well and won. No one from the Iowa Collegiate Hockey League could beat us. Games started to take us a little farther from the Des Moines Ice Arena: Western Illinois, Bradley, Illinois State. The schedule had opponents from other parts of the Midwest and beyond. Our record that year was another good one: 18–8–2. There might have been only one or two seasons in those early years that we didn't have a winning record, and that was because I was scheduling Division I NCAA teams. It was a fun ride, and our program developed.

I had planned to stay only a year or two at Iowa State. In fact, I finished my master's degree in one year and one summer before fall classes started in 1970. The PE department had expected me to stay on for two years as a graduate assistant. To finish in a year and one summer is unique, but I was fortunate in the way it turned out. Wally Hutchison was a professor in the department, and he said, "Hey, I'm taking a leave of absence to finish my PhD, and I need someone to fill in my position. You've developed quite a reputation in one year, Al. Would you be interested in taking my spot?" Sure enough, when Wally came back two years later, they made an opening in the department, so I had a permanent position, and I'm still in Ames more than fifty years after I got here.

Hilton Coliseum was already under construction when I came to Ames. There was a lot of enthusiasm for the project. A new football field to the south, eventually known as Jack Trice Stadium, was also part of the plan to refashion the eastern part of the Iowa State campus. Hilton Coliseum was to be a fourteen-thousand-seat home of ISU winter sports would have a much larger capacity for wrestling and basketball fans than the Armory. The building was also going to have room for big concerts and conventions. For Chris Murray and me, we saw a chance to bring hockey and ice skating in from the cold shadow of Beyer Hall.

"We view this in a very inclusive way, involving many activities and a large percentage of the students, faculty and even citizens of Ames," Chris wrote in an October 1970 letter to Dr. Richard Snyder, who was the director of that part of campus, known as the Iowa State Center. "The involvement should also be thought of as both viewing and active participation."

That's when I learned a lesson about administrators in higher education: if they don't want to do something, they can find ways to make it hard to do. In this case, I think they thought they could make me responsible for Hilton Coliseum not having ice equipment. They called me in and said, "Hey, we've got this possible alumni donor in Chicago. We just need $100,000, and we'll put ice in Hilton Coliseum."

I know what they were thinking: "This Murdoch guy will never get anything." But they hadn't counted on me knowing how to talk after years of listening to my dad. I went into Chicago and met with this guy who had his engineering degree from Iowa State. He was in a position where he could make a contribution like that, so I simply asked him for it. I said, "If you make the check out for $100,000, we'll have ice in Hilton." He wrote the damn check and gave it to me, and I drove back to Iowa State that same day. I said, "There you go. Let's get the ice in there."

The building opened in late 1971. There were miles of piping in the concrete floor to freeze the skating surface. I released a game schedule to the newspaper, noting that home games would be played at Hilton Coliseum. Tuesdays would be the days of ice availability for PE classes, public skating, youth hockey and intramurals starting at three in the morning and going until midnight.

It wasn't long before I was called in to the vice-president's office. I walked in not knowing what was going on. They had their big conference table in the middle of the room.

"Have a seat."

I think there were three different vice-presidents in there, a marketing person, the university foundation, all kinds of people.

"Murdoch, you know we can fire you right now?"

"What?"

"You released a poster that was inaccurate. You said all of these games were being played in Hilton Coliseum."

I said, "Well, I just made the assumption since the director of the facility said they'd be ready."

I didn't know what had occurred behind the scenes. They had hired Maury John from Drake as the new basketball coach. He didn't want ice at Hilton, and they had promised there would be no ice during basketball season. All winter, they came up with different reasons not to lay the ice. "Well, the equipment is not available. The boards have to be constructed. We have to decide what brand of ice resurfacer to buy," and so on. We went nearly a whole year with Hilton being open with no ice, and every hockey game from November to February was moved to Des Moines.

We were undefeated at Christmas and still hadn't lost until well into 1972. It was pretty impressive for a young team; that was the first season with an all-undergraduate roster, and we had a lot of freshmen. I would check with Dr. Snyder, and he would say, "You know, I don't know that we're going to get to play *any* of the games in here."

And I said, "Geez, couldn't we even get half the schedule in there?"

He slid the basketball schedule out in front of me and said, "I'm certain it won't be until their season is done."

Our only games after that point were to be held on a Saturday and Sunday against the Air Force Academy during the second weekend in March. I kept nurturing the Air Force series, saying, "Hey, this is going to be good for hockey. Air Force has an excellent team." Still, I kept the Des Moines Ice Arena available for backup.

Whether it was because the basketball team was done, the several articles about the ice situation printed in the *Iowa State Daily* or because the university wanted to see if all this equipment would really work, prospects for playing the March games on campus continued to improve. The rink was set up, and the first chance to skate at Hilton Coliseum came four days before puck drop. In between, they had to cover up the ice for an orchestra concert. Twenty-four hours ahead of our first game with Air Force, the Boston Pops played Hilton Coliseum.

By one point in February, we had pushed our record to 20–0, but we had run into trouble in the last few weeks of the schedule. We lost four out of the six games going into that last weekend. We were still practicing outside, and it was bitterly cold. Plus, the wear and tear was getting to our team as we played some tough opponents. Still, this is what we had been waiting for all year.

Vic Heyliger was the coach at Air Force. They had won over twenty games and were just coming off a win against Colorado College the weekend before. I wouldn't go so far as to say they were excited when they arrived, but they saw this facility with the boards and Plexiglas up, and it was probably better than what they imagined. There were 5,300 people there that Saturday night for a nine o'clock game. WHO-TV from Des Moines was there. I'll never forget seeing both teams lined up on the blue lines for the national anthem and cheerleaders out there on skates. It was a long time coming.

Dave Lee and Denny Francis scored goals for us, but a couple of others were washed out by the referee. That was the difference. Air Force won the opener 3–2. After it was over and the Academy team had gotten on the bus to go to their hotel, I went into their locker room to make sure there was no damage and nothing had been left behind. Written on their blackboard was "Beat Iowa State by 20 goals." They thought we were just some crummy country team. Well, they beat us that night, but we gave them more of a game than they had expected. They were definitely ready to go the next afternoon and won the second game 7–0. Still, it wasn't 20 goals.

That was the beginning of believing that we could really play anybody at any time. The whole attitude of the Air Force staff going into those games was that they were doing us a favor and helping the program at Iowa State grow. After the series was over, it was a whole different sentiment: "We want you back out to visit us in Colorado Springs. Can you play us next year? Pick a date." They wanted to kick our asses, and I think they did beat us pretty well at the Air Force Academy when we went. We played Air Force every two or three years for some time. The last series was part of a trip during which we also played the University of Denver. I bet Denver had six guys on their roster who had been drafted by NHL teams. They beat us pretty well, and then we had one day of rest and two more road games against Air Force Academy. We lost the first one in overtime and then beat them 5–3 on their ice.

I was a firm believer that if we played good competition on a regular basis, we would get better. The series against Air Force proved that. We did get better.

5

NEVER END ON A
PHILOSOPHICAL NOTE—CHARGE

I owa State always did well against teams from the Iowa Collegiate Hockey League. In my first season, we scored fifteen goals one night against Grinnell. The next year, we beat Graceland 18–0 during one game. The meetings with Drake were often closer, but the overall results were just as one-sided when it comes to wins and losses. For hockey to grow, we needed stronger opponents. There were some Division I teams, like Air Force, that would schedule us, but scholarship programs were usually in a conference like the Western Collegiate Hockey Association. During January and February, they were playing conference games.

This all helped lead to the formation of the Central States Collegiate Hockey League (CSCHL) in 1970. Iowa State was a charter member and still plays in the conference. Originally, the CSCHL included schools from Iowa and Illinois. It was a much better league with more teams like Iowa State that had recruited players who came from places where hockey was active at the youth level. The Central States League eventually flourished for decades in a roughly six-state area. That league extended all the way from Ames, Iowa, to Ohio University to Buffalo. At its peak, it grew to include fifteen or twenty schools from across the region, including major names associated with college sports, like the University of Illinois, Notre Dame, Northwestern and Purdue.

In the 1960s, the sports clubs at Iowa State and other schools around the country had actually encouraged students to compete alongside graduate students, as well as faculty and staff. There was an intermingling as part of the educational experience. Those of us who were a little older could provide some natural, informal education to underclassman. For hockey, that changed when we formed the CSCHL. We didn't exactly parallel NCAA rules, but we were darn close. Players had a certain amount of eligibility and had to be a certain age. They could not have played professionally and so on. It helped formalize non-scholarship hockey and probably helped some schools eventually move to the NCAA, but there was something lost with the change, too. It wasn't long before people would look at our procedures and say, "You're a club sport, aren't you? Not varsity?" I would tell them that we do everything the NCAA allows but with no scholarships. It turned out that was a huge positive, because many schools dropped NCAA Division I programs over the years due to a of lack of money. Scholarships were what cost the most, so to this day, Iowa State still has no hockey scholarships.

In the 1970s, we made some other alterations to how Iowa State hockey operated. One weekend, we played Mankato State, and we all drove in our cars to get there. Our equipment was the trunks of six or eight cars. There was one heck of a blizzard that weekend, and we were billeted with friends and relatives of players who were from Minnesota. That was when I considered the risky side of having guys driving their personal cars on icy roads through snowstorms. After that, we started taking charter busses and formalizing lodging arrangements. I have since discovered that a lot of schools from that time modeled their programs after Iowa State: practicing on more of a regular basis; paying attention to scheduling; having matching jerseys, socks and pants; traveling on coach busses. So, we were trendsetters.

Those years after we started playing in Hilton Coliseum have sometimes been called the golden era of Iowa State hockey, and we had some exceptional players. Doug Keseley was from Babbitt, Minnesota. He was an outstanding goaltender who probably should have been a Division I athlete. Mark Burch out of St. Paul was the captain for a couple of years. I would go to the Minnesota State High School Tournament every year, and I was aggressive enough to get players even though we weren't supposed to be recruiting there. I'd be down in the lower hallway talking to coaches and saying, "Well, if that player is available, I'd like to visit with him."

The high school coach would go back in the locker room and say, "Coach Murdoch is talking about you going to Iowa State."

"I am?" that player would say. And you know, sure enough, he would come down to Ames.

I am proud of the role I played in helping to bring ice equipment and hockey to Hilton Coliseum. *Author's collection.*

That was at a time when junior hockey had not fully developed. The Midwest Junior Hockey League was just getting started. In ten or fifteen years, a lot of these players would be going to the United States Hockey League for a season or two. I was able to steal quite a few players who probably should have been on a full-ride scholarship somewhere else if they'd had another year or two to develop. I think coming to Iowa State was attractive for them, because they could play at Hilton Coliseum in front of thousands of fans. Better than 50 percent of the students at Iowa State lived in residence halls. It was a captive audience, and I could call the president of a residence hall floor and say, "Hey, do you want a presentation?" Then I'd come out and talk about hockey and get the students excited to come to the games.

Occasionally, at that time, we would still run into difficulty with administrators signing off on the things we wanted to do. Iowa State is no different than other schools. There aren't many administrators or university presidents in the country who have played hockey. They are few and far between. There aren't many deans of students who have played hockey, so getting them on board with what we needed could be a challenge. Unfortunately for them, the lessons I learned were probably not what they would have hoped.

For example, this was around the time that Dan Gable won the gold medal in wrestling at the Olympics in Munich. Chris Taylor was a national champion heavyweight wrestler for ISU and won bronze in 1972. Of course, me being a marketer/promoter, at Hilton Coliseum between periods one night, we had a broomball game, with the two Olympic medalist wrestlers out on the ice. Somebody asked, "How did you get permission to have Gable and the big guy out there?"

I said, "You just ask *them*, and you don't tell anybody else."

So, that was part of my bad reputation around Iowa State: Murdoch would do stuff without asking.

At this time, I was fortunate enough to become acquainted with two men who were already successful hockey coaches. For all they had done to that point, Bob Johnson and Herb Brooks would go on to so much more. Of course, Herb Brooks was later the coach of the 1980 U.S. Olympic team and worked in the NHL after that. Bob Johnson also coached a U.S. Olympic team in 1976. For a time, he was the executive director of USA Hockey, and just before he died, Bob was the head coach of the Pittsburgh Penguins when they won the Stanley Cup in 1991. In the 1970s, Herb was with the University of Minnesota and would always tell me, "Iowa State's going to get there; it's just a matter of time." Bob was the same way at the University of Wisconsin, so they offered lots of encouragement and support.

One of the first times I met Bob Johnson was when we played the University of Wisconsin–Superior on the road up by Duluth. It was Christmas break, and instead of taking our team back to Iowa State and letting them go on a bender for the week until classes started, I figured we could pick up another game. I called Bob down in Madison, and he said, "We've got a second team here. You could play them, and that'll fill in your schedule."

I remember going to the big arena where their Division I team played and getting ready for the game. I looked behind our bench, and there's Bob Johnson. He said, "Oh, your team looks good," by which he might have meant our uniforms matched. We played pretty well and held our own, but I thought, "How many of these guys are from Wisconsin's Division I team?" It was probably only five or six. I continued scheduling games like that and telling our guys, "Even if we get our butts kicked, it's going to be good for us in the long run."

It was the same situation with Herb. We were playing somewhere in Minnesota, and he said, "Well come by and say hello." The Gophers had a JV team, too, and all of a sudden, Herb and Bob became my best friends, because I helped them by creating an opportunity for some of their marginal players to see more ice time.

In the '80s, Herb would say, "Al, here's the deal. I think there can be more varsity programs in the nation. The way I have it pegged, I'm going to help St. Cloud State go Division I."

And he did. He became their head coach for a year and said, "Iowa State is going to be next, right after St. Cloud, then Nebraska-Omaha is going to be the third one."

He did a stint as an NHL coach and then started scouting. That put him on the road a lot, and his territory included the Des Moines Buccaneers in the USHL. He'd call me as he was either going down to Des Moines or coming back and would stay overnight here in Ames. We'd have breakfast together, and he would ask what the Athletic Department was saying. "What can we do?" he'd ask. Unfortunately, between the basketball coaches not being thrilled about ice in Hilton and other challenges within the athletics department, he saw that we had some roadblocks, but he was certainly right about Nebraska-Omaha.

During the 1980s, Bob Johnson was leading USA Hockey, and by that time, I had started working with his summer hockey school in Aspen, Colorado. I went there twenty summers in a row to spend a week coaching with him and his assistant Grant Standbrook and a lot of other exceptional coaches. I got to know Bob, and he would teach me about the trials and tribulations of recruiting and fundraising and speaking. Of course, Bob was associated with the phrase "It's a great day for hockey," and he was always positive about everything.

Having a connection at the top of USA Hockey also created some unique opportunities. At one point, he said, "Al, I want you to go with me on this trip to Australia for their hockey association. It's in the summertime, so it won't conflict with anything. We'll take our wives."

I said, "OK, I think my calendar has the flexibility to do that."

We got there and were trying to offer them pointers on their youth programs. There was some type of seminar, and all of a sudden, he introduced me, saying, "Al, tell them about this." That happened on more than one trip, so it gave me the chance to talk to major hockey groups all over the world. Bob and Herb were good to me, and I consider them to be my strongest mentors.

Long before I went to Australia with Bob Johnson or took Iowa State on an overseas trip, I had the chance to travel to the Soviet Union in the summers of 1975 and 1976. Dr. Ed Enos was a professor and athletics director at Concordia University in Montreal. A decade later, he would be recognized by the pope for using sports to promote international understanding. The trips to Moscow in the 1970s were intended to exchange theories about coaching in North America with the Eastern Bloc. The first year, the group was entirely made up of Canadians, but the second trip was opened up to Americans. We had over one hundred people go, probably forty or fifty specializing in hockey, with the rest focused on track, swimming and other sports.

I still had my Canadian passport and said I would be interested in signing up for that first trip. It was a three-week educational seminar, and it was important that it be perceived as an equal exchange. One of the North American people would give a presentation, and then the Russians would give a presentation. My talk was about physical fitness and the use of video, and they seemed intrigued by the video idea. It was an absolutely excellent experience.

When they contacted me again about going back in 1976, I said, "There's a lot of coaches in the U.S. Can't you open it up to more than just Canadians?" When they did, I sent a personal letter to athletics departments all over the country, saying, "This is a good educational opportunity if you're interested in going." That's where I became good friends with Ron Mason, who eventually spent twenty years as a head coach at Michigan State. Between all these presentations, we were just sitting around waiting for the next speaker, so I would ask, "What are you doing with the power play? How do you defend Minnesota when they come to town—or Wisconsin?" It was an education in that way, too, and I brought a lot back to Iowa State in '75 and '76.

I also got to know Curt Bennett, who was a forward for the Atlanta Flames. We saw the sights and did some shopping around Moscow. Our Russian guides suggested we visit one of the popular saunas. The attendants would soak willow branches in the steaming water and then brush them lightly over your back. The brushing became a tapping, then a swatting. It certainly brought the blood to the surface. They followed that by having us jump into a pool of water that was so cold, I was amazed it didn't have ice floating on the top. Once we were out, we all drank a series of vodka toasts, and then the whole cycle began again. We were there for two or three hours, but when in Russia, do as the Russians do.

Anatoly Tarasov, the father of Russian hockey, was one of the lecturers during the seminar. At that time, Russians had a reputation for being dour and militaristic, but that wasn't Tarasov. He went up front with a bouquet of roses and invited our interpreter—an American girl—to come up. He said, "It's beautiful that they brought someone like you along," and then he gave her the flowers. He was definitely unique among the Russians. Tarasov had some drills that we took notes on, but what I remember most is that he had a nice way of thinking about life.

Since this was supposed to be an equal exchange, they would get into a jam sometimes and run out of North Americans to give presentations. Someone from our group would say, "Murdoch, you're a good talker. Get up there." So, I'd talk about dryland training at Iowa State. "Here's how you do an American push up." (You know, clapping your hands at the top before going back down to the floor.) I can only imagine the Russians writing this down in their notes: "The Americans are getting better because they're doing pushups and clapping between."

The second year I was there, I encouraged our group to take plenty of notes and to have an open mind. Not everyone did. I remember one coach saying, "There's nothing new here. What they do in the NHL is far better than this, and they'll never come close to us." Fortunately, I think most of the coaches from both sides approached these sessions with a good attitude: "Maybe he's got something to say. Maybe there's something unique or creative" (like clapping hands between push-ups). Silly stuff like that was almost more popular because those were things players hadn't heard of or done before. We could take those ideas back, incorporate them into our practices and keep things fresh. All in all, it was a great experience.

Bob Johnson was named the U.S. head coach for the 1976 Olympics. It was either at his camp in Aspen or after one of our games against Wisconsin's second team that he asked me to keep a date open for an exhibition game against the national team. In that era, Olympic preparation meant touring the country to play all sorts of opponents. Around the same time Bob came to Ames in early December 1975, the national team had games against the senior team up in Waterloo and professional teams in the IHL. As these games were played, the roster was eventually cut down to the group that would go overseas. The tour was also used as a fundraiser for USA Hockey, so making a stop at a big building like Hilton Coliseum was pretty attractive.

The Olympic hopefuls were current or former college players. Bob had coached some of them when Wisconsin had won the NCAA Championship in 1973. It goes without saying that they were very good. By the time they arrived at Iowa State, they had already played nearly forty games. Our record was 5–1–1. If there was one thing we had going for us, it was that the U.S. team had to fly from Madison to Minneapolis and then to Des Moines all on the day of the game.

There were plenty of good seats behind and across from the benches at Hilton Coliseum. The end seats were slightly obstructed. *Author's collection.*

It was a Sunday afternoon matchup. The buildup on campus had been very good. I took advantage of it: "You won't want to miss this. Be there, because chances are, they're going to medal at the Olympics. So, you'll have an opportunity to see them firsthand. And you'll see that Iowa State's program may not be at that level, but, by golly, we won't back down." There were about 2,800 people who came out, which is pretty good when you consider that it was the very end of the semester and finals were about to start.

Bob must have told his team, "Hey, we can't mess around with Iowa State." They were playing like the Olympics were the next day, and I'm sure Bob Johnson and Grant Standbrook said, "You got to imagine we're playing the Russians tomorrow, so skate like that for sixty minutes."

They scored nine goals on twenty-two shots in the first period. Four of those goals came in the last five minutes. They scored again forty-two seconds out of intermission. They looked like the Russians against us. Their passing was amazing, and we were chasing them all over the rink.

Dan Buffington was our goalie. He made thirty saves, and they scored on him twenty-two times. The quality of their chances was just too good. The score ended up being 22–1.

I think their players were upset that they allowed one goal. It was already 14–0 in the last minute of the second period. They said our goal was kicked in. Jerry Webb from Des Moines scored it on a scramble in front of the net. After play restarted, they came again, blasting away, and they scored twenty seconds later, just before the period ended.

After it was over, I told our guys, "Hey, learn from this, grow from this. And when you see highlights on TV from the Olympics, know you helped them get to that point."

Eventually, most of our players cleared out of the locker room. I was taking my time to cool down. Then I heard this knock at our dressing room door. It was Bob Johnson and Grant Standbrook. I felt like I had to apologize. "Sorry, guys. We should have given you more competition."

"Well, don't worry about that," they said. "Say, when you were studying with the Russians, do their goalies prefer to shuffle, or do they glide and stop at the other side of the crease?"

At the time, Americans were doing the glide and stop. The Russians were tending to do the shuffle. They wanted to know what I thought about the difference between the two and what was likely to be most effective. They asked me about whether the Russians really spent six hours on the ice each day and then trained for another two or three hours off the ice.

I said to myself, "Holy cow."

That's probably where I learned the most and got the most encouragement from Bob Johnson.

"Don't worry about it," he said. "You get beat. Big deal. The sun will still come up in the morning. Keep growing the game, and keep giving players the opportunity to be a part of hockey."

6

SELL, SELL, SELL!

Every week during hockey season, I would give a talk at a fraternity, sorority or residence hall floor to generate interest in hockey, and our crowds grew. We did not sell out Hilton Coliseum, because it could seat about twelve thousand for hockey, but there were many periods when we would average between four thousand and six thousand fans per game. From almost the very beginning, we had hockey cheerleaders. I got to know the people who ran the pep bands for football and basketball and said, "Hey, you better come out to the hockey games." The bands and the fans loved it: the action, the contact, the winning. How many times did we score goals in the last few minutes to win? That always brought the crowd back the next night, and we just about always played doubleheader weekends on Fridays and Saturdays.

Eventually, I ended up at the center of a tradition when we had a weekend sweep. In the late 1980s, the pep band realized "Don't leave after the Saturday game, because Murdoch will come out and wave to the crowd." When I did that, they would play the Paul Simon song "You Can Call Me Al." The guy at the scorer's table would know to put it on the speakers, and then the pep band would blend in. I would come out on the ice after both teams had gone to the locker rooms, and the fans who were still in the building would chant, "DOC-TOR HOCK-EY!" I'd start swinging my sportscoat over my head, and the fans would stay for that. It was kind of silly, but at the same time, it kept my adrenaline going, and the students loved it. I wanted to create that enthusiasm and fans who would want to come back to the next game, even if it was just to see what Murdoch would do next.

Left: From the earliest days of Iowa State hockey, cheerleaders on skates were always part of the action and excitement. *Author's collection*.

Below: The pep band always livened up Iowa State home games. They were also part of some famous ISU hockey traditions. *Bernie English*.

I was good at fundraising, and that was fortunate. I was not afraid to ask people for money, and that's what allowed us to eventually keep ice in Hilton Coliseum most of the time. We played more hockey in the Coliseum during the 1970s and '80s. They would cover up the ice for basketball and uncover it for our games. Of course, due to scheduling demands, there were times we couldn't play on a Friday night because of basketball, but we could play on Saturday. In the '70s, we'd end up playing at the Des Moines Ice Arena on Fridays and in Ames on Saturday.

For the most part, the trips to Des Moines ended in 1979, when we built an ice rink at the southern edge of campus. It was originally known as the Cyclone Area Community Center and initially was more or less a big steel shed built around and over the ice. One of my assistant coaches was John Russo. John had been a defenseman and captain for the Wisconsin Badgers in the 1960s. He finished his PhD in construction engineering and became a professor in that department at Iowa State. He said, "Hey, what we need to do instead of hoping for good outdoor ice north of Beyer Hall is just build a practice facility." That's how it started out.

We were on the campaign to raise money and came up with $110,000, plus donated materials and volunteer labor. Our team was out helping lay plastic piping alongside parents from the Ames Minor Hockey Association. They were out there raking sand and leveling things, and then, lo and behold, the building was ready for ice. Soon, not only did the building have a roof, but some of the creative people built additions with dressing rooms. The crazy part is that the fans loved that rink as much as they loved Hilton Coliseum, even though it didn't have the amenities. It could hold only about two thousand people at standing room capacity, and anyone who could find a seat was on the portable bleachers from the summer softball fields.

The manager of the arena was Wayne Kitchingman, who also helped me as an assistant. Wayne was from Ontario. His hockey career ended due to a shoulder injury he got when he was seventeen, but he went on to coach at the junior level and in the minor leagues.

Before the season, I'd be out selling advertising. Dasherboards were becoming popular. I said, "Hey, we should sell to beer companies. They'll put up $5,000 quicker than you can blink." I was told I couldn't do that, but then the City of Ames (which operated the building in partnership with ISU) sold beer company advertising. The city sold beer and operated the concessions. You'd better believe the crowd was pretty raucous on ten-cent beer night.

Without that building, hockey at Iowa State might have ended in the early 1990s. There were two major floods in Ames on the Skunk River and what is today known as Ioway Creek, one in 1990 and one in 1993. The first flood damaged all the equipment at Hilton Coliseum. The administration said, "Murdoch, you aren't going to be able to play in there next year. The boards are damaged, the plexiglass is broken and we're just not going to be able to play next season unless you can raise $150,000."

There were many businesses supporting us at that time, giving us money in the range of $2,000 to $5,000 for an advertisement in our game program or on the dasherboards. I was able to raise $150,000 fairly quickly. We hired a specialist from Winnipeg, Manitoba, who came down with a crew and rebuilt the boards and all the things that made hockey possible.

Then four years later, it happened again.

They called it a one-hundred-year flood. A flood of the century, but we had two of them within four years. The second one was very discouraging, because I had raised so much money, and I knew the second time it would cost even more. I hoped somebody else would step forward, but it didn't happen. Ten miles of piping is still in the floor at Hilton Coliseum. After several years, they cut the headers off where the pipes come together, and they cut the legs off the compressors to take them to salvage. That was the end of ice at Hilton Coliseum, and that was a low moment for me.

Even though we did not have hockey scholarships and our status on campus sometimes created other challenges, recruiting seemed simple to me. Early on, I drew from what I had seen during my two years at Bemidji State, where there were quite a few Canadian hockey players. Before I got to Bemidji and then for decades after, Bob Peters was the school's head coach. He was a good recruiter and was originally from Ft. Frances, Ontario, so his situation was similar to mine: a Canadian coach working at an American school. Bob's teams won NAIA championships year after year in the 1960s and '70s. They moved on to the NCAA and climbed from Division III to Division I, where the program is still active today.

I watched and learned the process: send out letters, maybe call recruits on the telephone, and then eventually invite them to come to campus. So, I replicated the letter writing at Iowa State, and sure enough, coaches from junior teams across Canada and the US would send me responses with two or three names. And then I'd call players on the phone and invite them to visit. Eventually, I'd go on the road. If my team had a week or ten-day break at Christmas, I'd go home to Canada, see family there, and make my way to the different arenas nearby.

If you want to recruit really good players, go to their games and then meet with the coach and player after the game. If I asked for the best two players and talked to them, eventually, I'd get some. So, I did that in Manitoba, Saskatchewan, Alberta and British Columbia. Over the years, I got a lot of recruits just because I was gutsy enough to go to their games and ask to meet with them. Of course, I would remind the Canadian recruits, "Yeah, I'm Canadian—from Manitoba."

The absence of athletic scholarships wasn't as much of a problem as you might expect. Being as creative as ever, I would teach prospective players how to approach the financial aid office. Even though there weren't hockey scholarships, there were financial aid packages. They could get guaranteed student loans or special scholarships if they were of a certain heritage. We got pretty imaginative in that regard.

I was also fortunate to earn a lot of trust from the hockey community. Bill Ward was a good example of that in 1989. I encouraged him to come visit campus while he was also being recruited by Wisconsin. The coaching staff there knew me, and they were honest with Bill. They told him, "Iowa State's a good school. You'd get a good degree there, and you'd get to play hockey with Al Murdoch. Here, you'd be on the fourth or fifth line, which means some games, you'll be watching from the stands. If you go play for Al Murdoch, you'll be on the first or second line, and you'll play regularly."

Bill Ward was one of many players who came to Iowa State in situations like that. They came and played for me for four years, and some of them—like Bill Ward—stayed on for another year or two after to help coach.

Recruiting to improve our team wasn't strictly limited to players. I mentioned selling advertisements for our dasherboards and our game program. That program grew from a four-page handout to have eight pages and then twenty pages. It was contagious, because it generated business for bars and restaurants and every other business in it. Of course, football and basketball had professional salespeople. For our sales staff, I would give talks to the journalism and marketing classes. I could make them laugh and see the fun of what we were doing; plus, it was an opportunity to work. Even though we didn't pay those people, it could go on their résumés that they sold advertising and wrote stories. Well, it got to be a pretty thick program.

Big events in the larger hockey world rippled to Iowa State. I don't think that it's any coincidence that hockey started in Ames around the same time the NHL was expanding and new teams were being established in Minnesota and St. Louis. As NHL games got nastier in the 1970s, we always had the philosophy that if two teams were fairly equal, the tougher team would win. Before long, fighting in college games led to an automatic ejection and maybe a suspension from the next game, too, but there was a period before that in which fighting was as common as a two-minute minor, so we had our share of those games.

The most substantial moment that brought attention to hockey was when Herb Brooks' U.S. team beat the Soviet Union at the 1980 Olympics. We were playing Chicago State on the road at that time. I remember getting updates on the score and how the U.S. team was doing between periods of our game. I think my players knew right away how much that game meant. It was a pretty thrilling time. It still ranks as the number one influence on the sport here in the United States.

Hockey players generally have a healthy sense of self-confidence. That might be truer of Dennis Vaillant than almost anyone else who ever played for me. He was a big, six-foot-three-inch-tall defenseman from Thunder Bay, Ontario, who came to Ames as a freshman in 1978. On the ice, Dennis was probably on the meaner side. He'd rather take your head off than do anything else. He made it four years with me, and I was proud of the fact that I kept him relatively stable during that time, and he got his degree.

At some point, he told me, "You know, I'm going to marry an Iowa State gal."

I thought, "OK, he's just a little rough around the edges."

As time went on, he would give me updates every once in a while: "I met her this morning, Coach."

"Met who?"

"The gal that I'm going to marry."

I said, "OK, Dennis. Good for you. Where'd you meet her?"

So, he gave me the story: "It was in the residence hall at breakfast. I was there before she came in, and so I sat at a table by myself. As other people came along to sit at my table, I said, 'No, no. Gotta wait.' And sure

Dennis Vaillant (*standing in the center*) pictured with fellow captains Rob Wilson (*left*), Glen Garnett (*right*) and Pete Bowman (*seated*). *Author's collection.*

enough, she came in, and I said, 'Come and sit here. You strike me as a very intelligent, very attractive person. Tell me about yourself.'"

Listening to this story, I imagined her thinking, "Who is this weirdo, Dennis Vaillant?" I think he said to her, even at that time, "You're going to be my wife after graduation." He was such an aggressive guy, but lo and behold, a couple of years after graduation, the two of them were married and went on to have many happy years together.

My own level of self-confidence around this time may not have had the same brashness, but it was healthy. I had been a tenured professor for several years and was well on the way to getting my PhD. Iowa State hockey was winning a lot of games and competing against some high-level opponents. For good measure, I opened a sporting goods store in Campustown on Lincoln Way. Sports Cellar was located under a restaurant, and customers would walk down there if they needed their skates sharpened or a new helmet and gloves. I also stocked some racquetball racquets and tracksuits, and I even sold trophies and awards. It was a third or fourth income, but it wasn't much. Nonetheless, it's what led to another important part of my working life.

Iowa State had career days, and the Continuing Education Center invited me to speak about running a sporting goods store while coaching and doing other things on campus. I was giving a presentation in one room, and there were other presentations happening as students went from station to station. The guy in the next room was talking about "twin career opportunities" with Life Investors. At some point, this presenter came over and asked, "What are you talking about?"

"I'm talking about sporting goods and where you can get skates sharpened when it's not a skate-sharpening town. What are *you* talking about?"

"I'm talking about twin careers. You know, we've got some coaches that have come on board to sell investments and insurance as a twin career while they're coaching."

"Oh, really?"

"Would you be interested, Coach Murdoch?"

"I might be."

Well, in about two days, they were recruiting me, so I started selling insurance and investments as a twin career. I got to the point that I would work two or three nights a week, earning additional income for my family. It allowed us to do some of the things we wanted to do. Eventually, after I learned the ropes, I found myself supervising other salespeople as far away as Carroll and Cedar Rapids. In fact, I enjoyed sitting down with people to talk about their retirement plans, and I was still doing that after I stopped coaching and retired as a professor.

I'm not sure exactly when, but at some point, all these pursuits began to weigh heavily on my family. My son Sean had been born in 1970. My daughter, Kerri, followed, and by the time Andrew came along in 1978, we were a very active family of five. When I got home, I sensed something was different. I'd fallen short of being a good husband who was around enough, and eventually, Noel found something different—someone more interesting or attractive who had more free time.

The end result was that I became a single parent for close to ten years. Ironically, Jane Reschly was a neighbor and had gone through the same thing with her former husband. Jane and I would run into each other at school activities. We had kids who were around the same age; her son Blake and daughter Amy were in the same schools as my kids. Neither of us were ever planning to get married again, so we were just good friends for about ten years.

Yet in that time, our relationship became a second chance for both of us, and we eventually became a family of seven. It's a story that's not nearly as bold or dramatic as Dennis Vaillant's engagement, but Jane and I have been married for over thirty years now, so it is a story that has worked out happily.

When you spend so much time together as a team, players and coaches start to regard each other as family. For all the good that comes with that, it creates hard moments, too. Larry Saal was an outstanding defenseman from Saskatchewan. He played at Iowa State for four years in the mid-1970s and then was an assistant coach for two more years. He would go home in the spring and summer to work his farm, so he came from a background similar to mine.

During his six years at the university, Larry could never pass statistics. He took it three times, and after the third time, he threw his books in Lake LaVerne. Now, Monty Brown—Monty the Barber, as he was known—was our good friend and had a shop just north of Lincoln Way, west of campus. All the guys would get their haircuts from him. Larry went over to Monty's Barbershop in the middle of the day after throwing his books into the lake. He knew Marty kept a bottle of whiskey in his back room, and Larry finished that bottle. He went home assuming that he would never get a degree from Iowa State, and eventually, he was back on the farm in Saskatchewan.

We kept in touch, and time passed. One day, Larry called: "Hey, Coach, I wouldn't mind seeing you one more time."

I said, "What the hell you talking about?"

"Well, I'm in the hospital. They say I've got terminal cancer, and I just wouldn't mind seeing you and Dan Buffington one more time."

Buffington had been our goalie. He and Larry became assistant coaches at the same time when they finished playing.

I called Buffington and said, "Buff, Larry's got cancer. He's up in Saskatchewan. We better go and cheer him up—get him the hell out of the hospital and tell him he can beat this cancer."

How do you get from Ames, Iowa, to Regina, Saskatchewan? There's next to no way to get there in a short period. Fortunately, through connections I had at Iowa State, I knew the pilot for the skydiving club. I called him and asked, "Can you get us Regina?"

"You bet."

Alan Murdoch
Head Coach

Al Murdoch begins his tenth year as coach of the "Exciting Cyclones." Mur-

Dan Buffington
Assistant Coach

Dan enters his third season as assistant coach for the ISU skaters. Dan is a

Larry Saal
Assistant Coach

Former Cyclone Larry Saal enters his first year of college coaching as an

Larry Saal and Dan Buffington became assistant coaches after playing for me on Iowa State teams during the 1970s. *Author's collection.*

I told him the story, and we got ready right away. I knew Larry still didn't have his damn degree. It's a long flight from Ames to Regina in a single-engine plane, so as the pilot was making arrangements and Dan was coming from Omaha, I called the registrar's office.

"Yeah, Al Murdoch here. Tell the registrar it's Dr. Murdoch calling."

John Sjoblom was the registrar. I had worked with him a lot through the years.

"Hello, Al."

I said, "I've got a guy who flunked stat three times. I want to have that course waived, and I want to get his graduation certificate, but before you answer me, he's got cancer. He's terminal. He's been given three days, and we're going to fly up and see him this afternoon."

"Geez, I don't know if we can do that, Al. Let me get back to you."

I said, "Well, we're flying out in about an hour."

He called me back and said, "OK, we're going to waive that course, Al. He'll get his degree."

And I said, "Any chance I could get the graduation certificate to take with me?"

"Jesus, Al—goddang it. Let me get back to you."

He called back fifteen minutes later: "Yeah, yeah. Come over here. Pick it up."

So, we got on the plane; it was Monty the Barber, Dan Buffington and I on this single engine plane with a pilot who flew skydivers, and we made it all the way up to Regina, Saskatchewan.

Having jumped from a plane with the ISU skydiving club (*pictured on the right*), I knew the right people to get me to Regina. *Author's collection.*

We walked into the hospital, and of course, old Coach Murdoch had to give a coach's talk.

"What the hell are you doing laying there. Get your ass up. We can beat this cancer or whatever the hell it is you got."

"No, coach. I'm ready to go."

"OK," I said. "Well, is there anything that you regret?"

And he said, "I regret not passing that goddamn stat course."

I said, "Larry, they waived that damn course. You're graduating, so get yourself healthy and get to graduation in a couple months. You'll walk across the stage in December at Hilton Coliseum."

He smiled a little and said, "Have Monty the Barber walk across for me."

I told him he'd be healthy enough. And after a little while, we left and flew back to Iowa. Larry died within a day or two.

Back in Ames, I called John Sjoblom.

"Hello, John. Al Murdoch here. Larry passed away. I know graduation is in December; he asked that Monty the Barber walk across the stage for him."

"Jesus, Al—goddang it. Let me get back to you."

He called back fifteen minutes later: "OK, Al, we're going to make an exception. The barber can attend graduation on Larry's behalf."

December came, and we were in Hilton Coliseum. Larry's family—his parents, wife and children—had come down for the ceremony. I don't think Monty had ever even taken a class at Iowa State. There he was in the robe and graduation cap, nervous as hell, but he walked across that stage and got that certificate for Larry Saal.

7

SECOND AT NATIONALS
IS LIKE KISSING YOUR SISTER

I was never more optimistic about Iowa State hockey becoming an NCAA varsity program than in 1987. In coordination with student government, we made a formal bid for the ISU Athletic Council to change our status. Over seven thousand students, staff, alumni and community members signed petitions in support of the transition. The annual hockey budget had reached $85,000 without any support from the athletic department, and we were sustainable at that level with ticket sales, advertising, donations, and fundraising. Other schools were shifting from non-scholarship to varsity, and I believed we were more than ready.

Max Urick was the athletic director. I asked him what it would take. His first objection: "You don't have scholarships." And I said, "We don't need them. We have been actively recruiting players for years without athletic scholarships." His next concern was our lack of a permanent rink, and I pointed out we had Hilton Coliseum, plus a second facility giving us the option for Friday night games here and Saturday night games there. It reached a point where he agreed I should make a presentation to the athletic council. When it happened, I thought it was one of the best presentations I had ever given.

At that point, the ISU Athletic Council included twenty-two or twenty-three people: a mix of faculty members, community residents and administrators. I felt the presentation was strong and well-received, but I didn't want to take a chance. A vote was planned for the group's next session a couple of weeks later. I scheduled one-on-one meetings with every member of the athletic council. "How are you going to vote?"

They did not all support the concept of ISU hockey going Division I. Still, I had twelve in favor and ten against as the next meeting approached. I arrived that evening, and the chairman asked, "Coach Murdoch, do you have anything you want to add?"

"No, I think we're ready to move forward. When I met with the members of the council, they seemed to have the information they were looking for."

"All right, we're ready for the vote."

Then a hand went up at the back of the room among a group of three or four ladies.

"We'd like to state something prior to the vote. I just want to emphasize that if you consider making another men's sport Division I, it will hurt women's sports, so be careful what you vote for." It wasn't much, but there was something cryptic in her tone.

The voting was done on paper as a secret ballot. Unlike a government meeting, the athletic council members did not have to state their preferences out loud. The votes were counted: ten in favor, twelve against. I have no idea who changed their mind, but I was absolutely crushed. Two people had flipped on an unsubstantiated argument: enhancing a men's sport would mean doing an unspecified injustice to women's sports. Maybe there was an implied threat that the university would be opening itself up to a lawsuit. Ironically, we founded a women's hockey program during the years that followed. They won an American Collegiate Hockey Association national championship in 2014.

It took me a couple of weeks to recover from the disappointment and surprise of coming so close, only to see the plan derailed so unexpectedly. By that time, I had been at Iowa State for eighteen years. Over the next three decades, the *Iowa State Daily* would write op-eds supporting hockey, and other fleeting arguments would be made why we should be promoted, but there was never another time we came so close.

Fortunately, there was another Murdoch on the brink of reaching Division I hockey.

My oldest son, Sean, was part of the Ames Little Cyclones team that won the Iowa High School Hockey League State Tournament in 1986. He had learned a lot from going on road trips with me and being able to skate almost anytime he wanted at the rink in Ames. After he graduated from high school, Sean played junior hockey in the USHL with the Des Moines Buccaneers for a couple of seasons. He had offers for partial scholarships from schools like Wisconsin and Notre Dame. Meanwhile, Iowa State took an international trip after Sean's first year with the Bucs; he had some free time, so I said, "Come with us. You'll be in shape when we come back." He had done the same thing a few years earlier when I had taken Iowa State to Europe.

That second international trip helped Sean tremendously, and all of a sudden, he was a top player for the Buccaneers. In the fall, they played during a heavily scouted USHL preseason tournament in Sioux City, and from that event, he committed to Brown University. An old high school football knee injury limited his college hockey career, but he spent four years on the team and graduated in 1994. After that, he even played a little bit professionally in Europe. His success in those years was definitely a thrill for me.

By the 1980s, non-scholarship programs were working together to host a national invitational tournament at the end of each season. Iowa State first appeared in 1985. The process of choosing the participating teams and host universities was relatively informal, and there was often some maneuvering by the most ambitious. During a meeting of coaches, the University of Arizona might say, "Hey, we'll host it next year." We did the same thing at Iowa State. North Dakota State and Penn State hosted it several times.

Of course, the host school was also one of the participating teams (usually, there were eight in the field). That school also didn't have the expenses and challenges of traveling to the event. Yet despite those advantages, I was among a lot of coaches who came to believe it was easier to win on the road due to the pressures of keeping everything organized. When we hosted the tournament, I had to make sure the officials had towels for the showers. If one of the team's hotel rooms weren't right or they were overcharged at a restaurant, the buck stopped with me. It was a whole different list of agenda items you had to deal with as the host. So, if you aspire to win a national championship, it's easier to do it on the road, even though you have the fans at home.

In 1986, we reached the championship game for the first time. It was the kind of team that a coach likes to have: they were impressionable, and if I said, "We're going to do this or that," they would listen. "Don't worry about the opposing team. The bigger they are, the harder they fall." We had only three seniors, but in some ways, our youth was an asset.

Arizona was the host, and they were the defending champions. Even though the NHL would not relocate a team to the state for many years,

Tucson had a minor-league club, and the city had a building that allowed hockey to grow at all levels. Leo Golembiewski was the University of Arizona coach and general manager. He had a substantial budget to work with, so his team was unique, and that showed. Still, this was one of the instances in which the host school didn't make the championship game; we met North Dakota State instead. I compare Arizona, Iowa State and North Dakota State as three of the top programs in those years. We each actively recruited and attracted a lot of junior players.

The final game went back and forth. North Dakota State had a little more depth through their four lines, and their coach, Jeff Aikens, was able to get the most out of his players. That was most evident in their power play and penalty killing systems. We tended to rely on our top five or six players for those units, but they could use their entire lineup, so they gradually wore us down. Still, our performance helped further Iowa State's reputation of being among the top teams in the country. Other schools were modeling their programs after Iowa State, North Dakota State and Arizona.

We were back in the championship game against NDSU in 1989, which was one of the years the tournament was held in Ames. When we lost games like this, it seemed like it was due to a hot goaltender who could keep them in it when we made a late push. Even with the experience we had, North Dakota State seemed to have a little more. They were deep, and I was careful not to match up our third and fourth lines with their first and second lines. Still, they came out on top again.

One of our best players at that time was a forward from Ontario named Rod Gold. Rod had a purebred rottweiler named Peevee, and his choice of breed would not surprise anyone who saw him play. He had been a junior player in Ontario, and I remember the coach from that team telling me, "I'm not sure you'd want Rod Gold on your team; he plays to win." I think Rod had been in a bind with the league in Ontario for playing on the edge of "dangerous."

I was the coach who took a chance on him. He turned out to be a great scorer in addition to having great toughness. When Rod was a sophomore, Alabama-Huntsville was transitioning from non-scholarship hockey to having an NCAA team, and we played them during a tournament in Detroit. It didn't take Huntsville long to figure out Rod Gold was our best player. They would shadow him whenever he was on the ice, so I got into a routine in which Rod would take a shift every forty-five or fifty seconds. I would say, "OK, Rod, you go out and center these two guys," and the opposing coaches had trouble keeping up, because he wasn't playing on one line. I think he scored three or four goals in that game, and we won 5–4. When the going got tough, Rod Gold would get going.

Rod was our senior captain when we played Penn State for the championship at Ohio University in 1990. It was one of the games that established a great rivalry with Penn State. Joe Battista had played there and then become their head coach in the late '80s. He has told me he watched what I was doing at Iowa State closely. When we played Penn State, I thought, "It looks like our team out there," and that extended beyond the ice to fundraising and other aspects of their hockey operation. During the 1990s and 2000s, they were exceptional and eventually made the move to the Big Ten and Division I NCAA hockey.

The 1990 championship game was everything you might expect. Both teams had battled hard during the tournament to get to the final. We were down 2–1 late in the second period and tied the game just before intermission. Penn State went back ahead early in the third, but we evened it up midway through the period. Eventually, they scored to make it 4–3 with about three minutes left. We didn't have time to make another comeback. It was our third runner-up finish in five years: two against North Dakota State and one against Penn State.

In addition to regular appearances in the national tournament, international travel was another Iowa State hockey tradition established in the 1980s. By international, I should clarify that I really mean outside of North America. We had always played quite a few Canadian schools: the University of Manitoba, the University of Winnipeg and my former school, Brandon University. Major junior players made up half of those teams or more, and the NCAA considers major junior hockey to be professional, so you know it was a high level of play. Those were great experiences for our team.

In 1983, we played at Alaska-Anchorage, and that's where I learned the most important thing about international travel with a sports team. Anchorage's longtime head coach Brush Christiansen gave me the secret: you've got to do an "inspection trip" in advance with your wife. "Sure," he said, "it's really a three- or four-day paid vacation, but believe me, wives need to get something out of this coaching lifestyle."

Iowa State's first trip to Europe came in December 1986 during the semester break. The four-game, ten-day tour took us through the Netherlands,

Preparing for the faceoff on Iowa State's first transcontinental trip. The dasherboard advertisements are a giveaway that we're playing in Europe. *Author's collection.*

West Germany and Austria. We played at the rink in Innsbruck where the 1976 Olympics had been held. That was a thrill for me and for most of our guys because they would have been old enough to remember those Olympic games. We won three of our four games, but the real highlights were what we did away from the rink: touring famous cities, learning about the local culture, skiing in the Alps. I was very insistent that education should be a huge part of a trip like this. I even encouraged our players, "Hey, talk to your advisor; get extra credit."

I aspired to take Iowa State on an international tour every four years. That would give every player an opportunity to go during their time in school, and that type of schedule provided time to fundraise for a trip like that. During the late '80s, we traveled a little more often. Less than two years after going to Europe, we were in Australia during September 1988 for the President's Bicentennial Cup Invitational. Of course, Australia is in the southern hemisphere, so September is the end of their winter. For us, it was the start of our fall tryout season, so it was an important training opportunity. There were four teams there, including Australia's national team and a touring team from Canada.

We had different adventures, like pulling the bus over at a kangaroo farm and learning how to throw a boomerang. We saw the Sydney Opera House and toured the capital in Canberra. We also brought back a story about a player who had almost been left behind. Steve Serek was a sophomore, and one morning, it was easier to sleep in than it was to get up and do the Murdoch dryland training. I'm a firm believer that if you aren't there when the bus pulls out, well, you're going to have to find out where the bus is going and catch up. In this case, it was also a travel day between cities, but Steve found a way to catch up with us before we got back to Sydney for our flight home.

That's not the wildest story about a bus on a cross-border trip, which happened several years later. We were on the way to the University of Manitoba. I contacted immigration and said, "How tough is it going into Canada these days?" They suggested sending a list of players and staff with social security numbers so they could double-check their backgrounds in advance. It turned out we had four players on our team who had been arrested for something in their lifetimes. It was pretty minor stuff, but it was on their records.

What we didn't know is that we had a problem that involved our bus driver. He had been in some real trouble, and we didn't find out until we were at the border. "You're not going to Canada," they told him.

Brian Wierson was my assistant coach, and I said, "Brian, come here. You're the driver now."

He was more than a little surprised: "I've never driven a bus in my life, Coach."

I said, "It's easy. You just start it, put it in gear, and go. Don't tell anybody you don't have a bus license." We had to be up there for a game early the next day.

Brian said, "Coach, will you sit here up front in the copilot seat, just in case."

I said, "Listen, it's easy. You just shift gears and go."

So, we walked to the bus door and stepped off. The border agent was outside, still telling the bus driver he couldn't go to Canada and directing him to a motel half a mile down the road.

Then he turned to me, "Your backup driver, Coach, what's his name?"

"Brian—Brian will take the bus to Winnipeg."

When I had the chance, I whispered, "Just walk fast and don't make eye contact."

We got back on, and the agent said, "You've got everything you need?"

An Iowa State team photograph taken under the flags of countries participating in an Australian hockey tournament in 1988. *Author's collection.*

"Yeah, we're good. Close the door, Brian."

He did really well, driving us all the way to Winnipeg. We got there, and he said, "Coach, did I do OK?"

"Yeah, you did OK—other than in Altona. There's a railroad track going across the road, and buses are supposed to stop there before going on. You just shot through it at sixty miles an hour."

"Oh, shit."

"It's OK. There weren't any police cars around."

Brian Wierson: assistant hockey coach and emergency international bus driver.

Each spring, an event called the Chicago Showcase brought all-star teams of high school players together for a week at one rink. Many of these players came from places that were outside the hockey mainstream, and they hadn't been scouted by colleges or junior teams. The Showcase became a regular recruiting destination for me and many coaches from non-scholarship programs. While we were there in 1991, eight or ten of us got together and said, "Hey, why don't we have a legitimate national tournament?" That was the basis for forming the American Collegiate Hockey Association.

Membership in the ACHA ensured that we were all playing by the same rules for recruiting and eligibility. Teams in the Central States Collegiate Hockey League were already operating at a high level and so were programs like Arizona, North Dakota State, and Penn State, but as more teams got involved, the ACHA gave us a basis for operational standards. You couldn't play in the ACHA unless your helmets, pants, jerseys, and everything else matched. We grew very quickly, with seventy to eighty teams in the early years to more than five hundred within a couple of decades.

I was the first president of the association. It was important for me to make sure players were taking the right number of credits and were academically eligible. We didn't pretend to be the NCAA, but it was important to have scholastic credibility. My philosophy had always been: recruit the outstanding students; those outstanding students can get academic scholarships, and eventually, they'll be the ones with degrees in business and architecture and other prominent fields who will be able to support our programs in the future as alumni. Even now, I don't believe the ACHA should be satisfied with five hundred teams. I think there could be eight hundred or nine hundred in the country.

On the ice, I pushed to use the same playing rules as the NCAA. It was important to present the game at a high level, and ticket sales were a significant part of funding for many ACHA programs, particularly those that had already established an engaging atmosphere. One of the things I advocated for immediately was to not undersell what we were offering to recruits or fans. I said, "There are some things that will sink your boat quicker than you can blink: don't refer to yourself as a 'club.'" What's a club? It's a social organization. University administrators like to call you a club to try to put you down. At Iowa State and other schools with serious ACHA programs, we were *teams*, so I would always use that term.

Almost immediately, the ACHA had two competitive divisions, which had the effect of raising the level of play. Iowa State and other schools with ACHA Division I teams could also field a Division II squad. One of the problems when playing an NCAA program was depth, because schools like Wisconsin or Minnesota had four of five excellent forward lines. Against one of those programs, we had to match them by playing our first line, then second line, back to the first line, then the third line, and back to the first line again. It's hard to keep that up for sixty minutes against an opponent that is rolling four lines equally. Having a second team gave us the chance to recruit a little deeper and move players up as they developed.

At Iowa State, I had coaches who could take charge of our Division II team. I would encourage them to come to the Division I practices so they could use the same drills and coaching techniques. Our Division II team became pretty good. Of course, there were some players who carried a chip on their shoulders and felt they should have been on the Division I team. I wasn't necessarily "Mr. Popular" when the rosters were finalized. I told the Division II team, "Play well, and you may move up." I was a believer that the more people who were wearing the Iowa State jersey, the better. It wasn't long before Iowa State and the ACHA added a Division III classification. Two divisions for ACHA women's hockey were established in the early 2000s. At its core, the basic principle of the association was: let's give people the opportunity to play, and let's do it while they're also getting a great education.

8

I WANT TO COME TO AMERICA

owa State won the ACHA's National Championship in 1992. The beginnings of that achievement stretched back more than a year earlier and to the other side of the world. I was told China hosts an international tournament in Harbin during the city's annual Ice Festival. I wrote a letter and made some telephone calls, and we were invited along with teams from the Soviet Union and other parts of the world. Remember, there was a lot happening in the news at this time. The Berlin Wall had recently fallen in 1989. The Tiananmen Square protests were held that same year. Russia was changing. Iraq had invaded Kuwait, and as we left for China in January 1991, America was on the brink of the Gulf War, so it was a memorable time to be involved in international athletics.

When we played in tournaments, we would always schedule an exhibition game or two. In this case, the first of those games was held against an old friend. Jim Robinson had been an Iowa State hockey captain back in the early 1970s. By this time, he was an architect or engineer in Hong Kong. He invited us to play against his adult men's team in the city. There's not much to say about the game itself (we won handily), but it helped with the time change. Jim also gave us an introduction to the culture, and it was great for our players to know an Iowa State alum who was working successfully on the big buildings in Hong Kong.

I can't say enough about the importance of having good assistant coaches when making a trip like this. At the time, Dick Williams was one of the coaches on my staff. He had become a golf pro in Marshalltown after playing college hockey at Penn State. He was an excellent assistant and helped oversee the team, heading off trouble before it happened. Dick could even play piano and led the singing as we kept ourselves entertained during the evenings.

We saw a lot of China over the next few days. Some of the trip was made by train, which unexpectedly required a seat and an extra ticket for our skate sharpener. We flew the last leg into Harbin, which is located far to the north and is bitterly cold in winter. The basis for the ice festival there is the big chunks of ice that are cut from the river to make ice sculptures. Once those blocks were pulled out, we saw local people diving into the freezing waters and swimming, and that was definitely something that amazed our players. The outgoing nature of our team connected with people. Our guys would gather in the hotel after games; they'd sing songs and welcome Chinese people to join them. As part of these international games, it was also always custom to exchange pins. I've got pins from all over the world from what are often referred to as "friendship games."

That name can be somewhat misleading, because the games weren't always friendly. At one point, I was visiting with members of the Chinese and Russian coaching staffs in the coffee room. We made our way back toward the rink, and there was a fight on the ice before the period had started. My Chinese counterpart was saying, "No, no, we cannot fight. This is a friendship game." The Russian on my other side was saying, "This is very good. We need practice in fighting."

Like they had during my earlier visits to Europe and Australia, some of my family was able to participate in the China trip. My sons Andrew and Blake served as the stick boy and equipment manager, respectively. My daughter Kerri was among the cheerleaders. Years earlier, Kerri had been on skates almost as soon as ice opened to the public at Hilton Coliseum. She was one of the first kids to take lessons there from Marilyn Muhlenpoh, who had once been part of traveling ice shows. Kerri had continued to figure skate at the Cyclone Area Community Center and all the way into adulthood when she got involved with a synchronized skating club. Even though she attended Iowa instead of Iowa State, I think she always enjoyed being a skating Cyclone hockey cheerleader when the opportunities came up.

In China, our cheerleaders were performing routines in a stadium packed with eight thousand people; needless to say, that was a lot different than what the locals were used to. The normal situation was having a very reserved and respectful crowd. To enforce that atmosphere, the military was in the building—and armed—facing the fans from the edge of the rink. The

Assistant coach Dick Williams (*left*) and I are dressed for the cold, but a Harbin Ice Festival participant is dressed for a swim. *Author's collection.*

I always believed our international trips should include cultural experiences like our stop at the Great Wall of China. *Author's collection.*

soldiers were definitely not happy with the cheerleaders, who were trying to get the crowd to do the wave and be more active. When I reflect on that situation, which was tense for a few minutes, I think it was definitely a reminder to appreciate the freedoms we have in North America.

The way we played was more physical than the prevailing international style at the time. That led to a lot of penalties. It was one of the major reasons we finished fifth. Still, the games there showed that we could play at a high level against opponents from anywhere in the world.

Of course, the local favorites were the Chinese national team. They were fairly good, but we were better and won our game against them. Watching from the bench, I thought, "This is unique," because they had one player who stood out as being far better than all the others. After the game, we went into our locker room. I was giving a postgame talk—anyone who played for me knows I always had to give a postgame talk—and then, suddenly, there was someone tugging on my shoulder.

I said, "What are you doing? I'm talking to the team."

"Coach, I want to come to America."

Anfu Wang was the established star on the Chinese national team. By 1991, he was already several years older than the rest of our players, but from a very young age, he had been the most valuable player of his country's national program. One of the customs for teams that won in international competition was that the Communist Party rewarded the outstanding players by giving them a house. Anfu literally had several houses for all he had accomplished.

Even still, he wanted to come to America for the chance to play in the NHL.

When he visited our locker room and asked to come to Iowa State, I said, "OK."

It took me most of 1991 to get through the red tape. Finally, he was released to be a student in North America. Iowa senator Chuck Grassley's office helped me get the correct visa. That was when I learned how good Anfu really was. China recognizes its leading athletes across all sports each year. Hockey players are rarely included, but he was among the group of about ten athletes honored throughout the entire country that year. It was something that caught the attention of the U.S. authorities and helped his application.

Anfu Wang's skillset was remarkable, and his arrival in Ames was a key milestone on our way to the 1992 ACHA National Championship. *Author's collection.*

At five feet, eight inches tall and 170 pounds, he was undersized, yet he was an exceptional skater and stickhandler. Anfu also had a unique shot; his wrists were so quick, he could tip his own shot with the toe of his stick. I don't know how he did it, but he did, and all of a sudden, the puck was in the net. Goaltenders had trouble tracking the shot, and more than once, I saw them react as if to say, "How did he do that?" A lot of guys tried to replicate it, but nobody could.

After we won the 1992 championship, I encouraged Herb Brooks to take a look at Anfu. Herb was working for the New Jersey Devils at that time and was definitely skeptical that a player from the ACHA could be successful as a professional. Still—maybe as a favor—he made the arrangements along with Robbie Ftorek, who was also coaching in the Devils organization. Ftorek took Anfu down to the ice with a bucket of pucks, and after all those years of practicing in China, Anfu's shot was remarkably accurate. Within a few minutes, Ftorek reported back to Herb, "Geez, this guy is good. He's *really* good."

They decided to give him a shot in a preseason game with their farm team, the Cincinnati Cyclones. Unfortunately, it was one of those games in which the players were trying to show how physical they could be in order to impress the coaches. Both benches were emptied, all the players were fighting on the ice, and only one player stayed on the bench. Anfu didn't know what they were doing out there. What was this? So, he didn't make the team, and they sent him back to Ames.

When Anfu first arrived at Iowa State in December or January during the 1991–92 season, I remember he came to me asking about a chance to work at the university bookstore in Campustown.

"They will pay me money," he said enthusiastically.

"Go for it."

So, in the beginning, here was this world-class athlete just carrying boxes of books and unpacking them. But no matter what, he was always very positive. His teammates watched out for him and kept him out of trouble. Coming to a new place, especially where everything is so different, can be difficult, so being part of a team sheltered him from some of that, and he never developed any bad habits that sometimes come with culture shock.

Anfu's wife was an outstanding gymnast and was pregnant back in China. It took another six months to get all the paperwork done, but she arrived in time to deliver their son. Anfu was playing hockey and attending classes, and by this time, he had moved on to working at Hy-Vee. The store's Chinese food area became its most profitable department for several years, because Anfu introduced his own authentic family recipes. He really hadn't been in Ames long, but with his exceptional athletic status from China, it was like his U.S. citizenship application was fast-tracked. He, his wife and their two children are still in Ames today, now working as successful restauranteurs with their own business. It's a one-of-a-kind success story for them and for Iowa State hockey.

We had started the year without Anfu. We were a young group with a lot of freshmen and sophomores. Under the circumstances, I told the *Iowa State Daily* in October that our goal was to be .500, but that team was willing to listen to me. They came to believe what I told them. You've got to be in good shape. You've got to go to class. You've got to do the right stuff. The buy-in started with dryland training and the mud run. They would listen, even when we didn't have overwhelming success early. They may not have had the most talent among my teams at Iowa State, but they listened and believed.

I held ninety-minute practices and always had incentives so the team would get the conditioning without knowing they were being conditioned. The first half hour was focused on individual skills. The second half hour was filled with team skills: two-on-one, three-on-two drills. There were power play and penalty killing segments, and I always took pride in our penalty kill. We would skate at the end, depending on how hard they worked during the rest of practice. Some days, we wouldn't touch a puck during the last ten or fifteen minutes. Some ACHA teams practiced twice a week; I practiced every day except Sunday. I would tell them, "If we can stay close to a good team through the first and second periods, we've got it. We're a third period team, because we're in shape."

Scott Geiger was our senior goalie from West Des Moines. He had been one of the best high school players in Iowa before joining the Des Moines

Buccaneers, and he did it while battling through knee problems. Mark DiGidio was the other four-year player. He was an undersized defenseman from Cooper High School in the Twin Cities. We did have another senior: Danny Kasperski was from Saskatchewan, and had been recruited to Iowa State with a full ride scholarship as a pitcher for the baseball team. It was his fifth year, and his eligibility was up for baseball. Danny had played junior hockey back home and wanted to play for us during his last year of school.

Our captain was actually a junior. Brian Williams was an outstanding student in mechanical engineering and was very hardworking on the ice. He had grown up outside Chicago and played youth hockey there. Brian was a defense-oriented defenseman. His coaches in Chicago didn't consider him a goal-scoring threat and parked him on the blue line. Whatever his game lacked in flash, Brian could emphasize the philosophies that I espoused and had a way of guiding his teammates away from bad habits. He was a good one, and in fact, he was one of my favorite captains.

Bill Ward was another leader on that team. He had been playing prep school hockey a few years earlier when he chose Iowa State over Wisconsin, but then he missed parts of two college seasons. In 1991–92, Bill was a redshirt sophomore from an eligibility standpoint, but he was still an assistant captain. Finally fully healthy, he became our top scorer and repeated that feat each of the next two years. In fact, his 107 points in 1992–93 were an Iowa State record. After the 1993–94 season, Bill was awarded the Bob Johnson Trophy, the equivalent of the Hobey Baker Award in NCAA hockey, as the most valuable player in the ACHA.

Another player who merits an introduction is Peter Jervis. He was our backup goalie from Upstate New York. Peter was wedged between Scott Geiger and Kyle Geiger, Scott's younger brother who was already attending Iowa State as a freshman goalie. Peter might have been a little larger than normal for the time, but at six feet tall, he was small by today's goaltending standards. To watch him on the ice or while going through training, he was average. Still, it takes a lot of intestinal and mental fortitude to be a backup goaltender. That's what he was, and it was a role from which he made a vital contribution.

We struggled with consistency during the early parts of our schedule. Before Thanksgiving, we allowed at least ten goals during games against three different opponents. Meanwhile, we scored in the double digits four times before Christmas. At one point, our record was 7–11–1. Our eighth consecutive invitation to the national tournament was definitely in jeopardy at midseason. Anfu's first game in early January was part of the upswing:

an eleven-game winning streak. We lost our last game of the regular season to North Dakota State and later lost 3–2 in overtime against Illinois during the CSCHL tournament championship game. Still, we had done enough to qualify for the postseason with a 20–15–1 record overall and a 19–6 mark against ACHA programs.

Penn State hosted the 1992 ACHA Tournament. The eight qualifying teams were broken into two divisions. Each school was guaranteed three games, all played between Wednesday and Friday during the final days of February. The winners of the two pools were then matched up for the championship. On our side of the field was Eastern Michigan, Arizona and North Dakota State. Michigan-Dearborn, Penn State, Ohio and Navy were in the other division. You needed to have a good record to get to the final, but our first two games left us in a tenuous position.

We had beaten Eastern Michigan twice during the regular season, then again during the CSCHL tournament. At nationals, we were ahead 6–4 in the third period but allowed two goals in the last four minutes. In order to keep the tournament on schedule, there were no overtimes or shootouts in the preliminary round, so the game ended in a tie, with both teams earning one point toward advancing. The next day, the same thing happened, only it was worse. We coughed up a four-goal lead to Arizona and finished in a 7–7 tie.

Scott Geiger was our goaltender during the first two games. He had played more throughout the year and led us to a lot of success, but toward the end of the season, the players were just exhausted. They gave it everything they had, but I could tell, there wasn't much left to give. So, Peter Jervis went in for the game against North Dakota State. It was one of those calculated risks a coach takes. The way the other games had played out, we could still get into the championship if we won on Friday.

North Dakota State had beaten us for the championship in 1986 and 1989. Earlier in the 1991–92 season, they had swept us during a two-game weekend in Fargo. They had stopped our eleven-game winning streak at the end of the regular season by beating us in Ames. We didn't let it happen again, and we didn't let another late lead slip away. Dick Hill scored shorthanded in the second period to give us a 1–0 lead. It opened up as the game went on; Anfu Wang and Bill Ward each had a pair of goals. Peter Jervis held NDSU to two, and we finished the win we needed, 7–2.

IOWA STATE

1992 ACHA NATION

(left to right) Row 1: Scott Geiger, Tom Armitage, Dan Kasperski, Bill Ward, Brian Willi
Row 2: Assoc. Head Coach Dick Williams, Chris Peterson, Joe Shaffer, Aaron Laaveg,
Head Coach Al Murdoch; Row 3: T. J. Reinch, Chris Wherity, Todd Krollman, Joe Baxt
(Photo taken by Asst. Coach Rick Hahn)

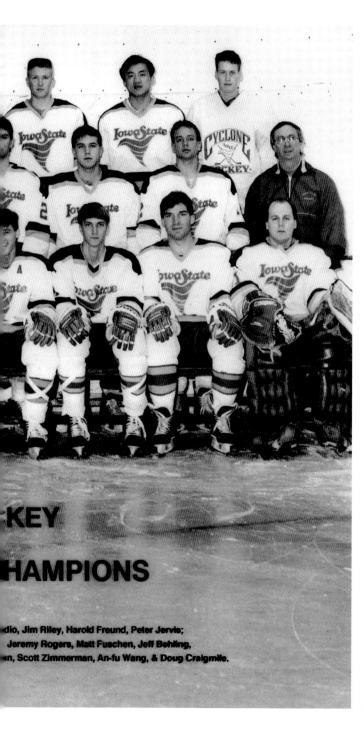

KEY

HAMPIONS

...dio, Jim Riley, Harold Freund, Peter Jervis;
... Jeremy Rogers, Matt Fuschen, Jeff Behling,
...n, Scott Zimmerman, An-fu Wang, & Doug Craigmile.

The 1992 ACHA
champions were
underdogs who
beat Michigan-
Dearborn 5–3 in the
championship game.
Rick Hahn.

Michigan-Dearborn was next. The Wolves were the top overall seed in the tournament. They had lost only three games all season, although one of those losses had been to us in Ames, 5–2, at the beginning of February. Michigan-Dearborn had been an NCAA Division I program during the late 1980s. Even though the college had brought the team back to non-varsity status, they honored the scholarships for those varsity players who hadn't yet graduated. A half dozen or maybe eight players on their team were still scholarship athletes.

Penn State's Ice Pavilion had a little more than 1,000 seats and could have held 1,400 at full capacity. There might have been 75 or 100 actual Iowa State fans in the building who had driven or flown in for the tournament, but the place was pretty well packed for the championship game. I looked around and thought, "Who could all those people be?" Well, they were Penn State fans who were disappointed that their team wasn't in the Saturday night final. Michigan-Dearborn had beaten Penn State, so the crowd was ready to get behind whoever was playing against Michigan-Dearborn. They adopted Iowa State as the underdog.

I knew we had to do something unique. Dave Szymanski was the Wolves' leading goal scorer, and I told our players, "We definitely can't give him any breaks at all. We've got to put a body on him." Todd Krollman was a freshman from northern Minnesota, and he took that to heart to make one of the game's biggest plays during the very first shift. The first time Szymanski touched the puck, Todd stepped up and put a perfect body check into him. It was a hard, clean hit. Szymanski had injured his shoulder earlier in the season, and I could tell that hit affected him for the rest of the game. He still played a regular shift, but he wasn't the same player.

Anfu Wang scored the first goal during a power play. Michigan-Dearborn tied it, and that was how it went. Joe Aho was their goaltender, and he was outstanding, but I thought if you could get him to make the first move— dropping a shoulder or giving a head fake so he would commit one way or the other—it would create opportunities. Anfu scored like that again, but the game was tied 2–2 by the second intermission. All the while, the Penn State crowd was getting louder and louder, with all the chants they would use for their team changed to cheer for Iowa State. For years after that game, I told Penn State coach Joe Battista that his fans cheered louder for Iowa State that night than they ever had for Penn State.

"I know they did," he would say.

Four minutes out of the second intermission, a sophomore named Joe Schaffer scored our go-ahead goal. Anfu added his third of the game just past the middle of the period, and we were ahead 4–2. But with five minutes to go, Szymanski made the score 4–3. I told the team that we were going to run short shifts. You can't stay on the ice for too long with an exceptional team. Anfu would come off, saying "Change, change! Quicker, quicker!"

In our net, Peter played the game of his life. He could make the initial save and be down but still cover at the bottom half of the net. Michigan-Dearborn players were smashing his glove and blocker with their sticks, but Peter would just hang in there, making all kinds of desperate saves. Brian Williams was back there trying to protect the crease. He'd find ways to clear the puck without taking an icing call, or he'd give Peter enough room to freeze the puck for a whistle. The shifts were thirty or forty-five seconds long, with new players coming on the ice, even though they weren't fresh anymore.

We were into the last minute, and we might have all been wondering if it was just a matter of time. Was this going to end the same way our games against Eastern Michigan and Arizona had? We just weren't as deep. Could we win if the game went into overtime? Michigan-Dearborn had pulled Aho for an extra forward. Dan Kasperski was on our bench, and I said, "If you get it, don't try to score the length of the ice. Carry it all the way to the net."

That's what he did with twenty-five seconds to go for an empty net goal. We were ahead 5–3 when someone poured a bucket of Gatorade over me. That was the final score. Peter Jervis made thirty-one saves and was named to the all-tournament team, along with Brian Williams. Anfu was the tournament MVP. We were still celebrating as we went for pizza after the game and as we got onto the bus for the fourteen-hour ride home. We might even have been celebrating when we got back to Ames (a crowd gathered there to meet us), but our bus's engine blew outside of Chicago. It took hours to get a replacement. We didn't make it home until early Monday morning. Still, even with a broken bus and being coated in sticky Gatorade film from the night before, it was one of those unique times in life when everything was good.

9

CYCLONE HOCKEY,
WHERE WINNING IS A WAY OF LIFE

Attendance was a little higher than normal at our season-ending banquet in 1992. In addition to players and parents, the event attracted a few friends, classmates, and fans. There was a lot to celebrate. Of course, winning the ACHA championship renewed the discussion among our supporters about whether Iowa State hockey should become an NCAA program. I told the *Iowa State Daily* that varsity status was the next aspiration, and "if it takes me another twenty-three years like it took me to get this [national championship], I'm not sure I'll live that long. But that's what I keep striving for." However, the timing was unfortunate. At that point, the athletic department was considering eliminating sports due to budget constraints. Within just a couple of years, Cyclone men's tennis and men's gymnastics disappeared. Baseball lasted only a little longer.

After winning the ACHA title, it was easier to talk to recruits from all over the world, and that's what I did. I had always been willing to talk to anybody at any time, but having national championship credentials helped open the door with some players and their families. We had more campus visits, and I was going on the road more. I am sure that championship contributed on some level to bringing many of the outstanding players who were part of Iowa State hockey over the next decade.

Yet winning in 1992 was no guarantee of success in 1993. Anfu Wang, Bill Ward, Peter Jervis and most of the roster remained intact. Still, it just didn't come together the same way at the end. Bill Ward scored an outstanding 107 points and earned his first nomination for the Bob

Bill Ward chose Iowa State and then became the first player from our team to win the Bob Johnson Award. *Author's collection.*

Johnson Award. We were runners-up in the CSCHL and finished fourth at nationals. That year, North Dakota State was a rare example of a host team that won the title.

Iowa State hoped to accomplish the same thing in 1994 after our bid to host the tournament was accepted. Both our team and the ACHA had a lot of credibility in Ames at the time. Our entire organization had adopted the Murdoch techniques for publicizing. At every chance, we would say, "It's going to be the number one event in the nation, with outstanding athletes from all over the country." The pitch was enhanced by the ACHA's announcement in 1993 that the national champion would receive the newly established Murdoch Cup, which had been named in my honor as the association's first president. I hate to say it, but I did so much marketing and campaigning over the year in preparation for the tournament that I was glad when it passed. We played and had good crowds, but we were also-rans once again.

Bill Ward's raw statistics did not match his 1992–93 numbers, but with thirty-eight goals and sixty assists, he was still exceptional. He continued to lead our team while wrapping up his coursework in marketing. This time, ACHA coaches rewarded him with the Bob Johnson Award. He received the trophy at the same dinner where the Hobey Baker Award was presented.

It had been almost four years since our team had gone to China, and 1994–95 meant it was time for a long-awaited overseas trip. Our players raised over $2,000 apiece, and we flew to Russia just after Christmas. We lost twice in Moscow and twice in St. Petersburg, but the games themselves were almost an afterthought for all that was packed into eleven days. It started right from landing after ten hours in the air. We were tired as blazes but went right to the Bolshoi Ballet. I wasn't sure we would keep our eyes open. More than anything about the performance, I remember the intermission. It was like everyone in the theater went to the escalators at top speed and downstairs for champagne. Then they charged back just as quickly to be seated before the next act. Russians could act very stern, but many we met were very nice, friendly, wonderful people. St. Petersburg is one of the most beautiful cities in the world, and for art and culture, there's far more to see there than in Moscow. It was another trip my family was able to participate in. My daughters Kerri and Amy were cheerleaders, and young Andrew played for us, even though he was only sixteen and still in high school.

By the mid-1990s, Iowa State was enjoying an influx of local players from Ames. Brian Wierson and Rusty Crawford were freshmen that winter and would make substantial contributions in the years ahead. Brian was versatile; he could play anywhere, any time (and even drive a bus, as we found out years later) but was primarily a forward. Anything he lacked in ability, he made up for in hard work and hustle.

During one game in Chicago, Brian was hit so hard, the trainers and on-site paramedics thought he had broken his back. They took him off the ice on a stretcher. After a stay in the hospital there, he returned under orders not to do anything for a couple of weeks. Brian couldn't stay on the sidelines. He was back on the ice for noncontact activity within a few days and back to practice a day or two after that. His determination was inspiring to the rest of his teammates.

Rusty was a defenseman, an excellent student, and a good all-around athlete. I recruited him at the high school state tournament in Waterloo with several other Ames players. They were good, and I said, "Hey, come to Iowa State. You'll get to play as much hockey as you want." And they played for me for four years. Rusty's familiarity with Ames also provided additional benefits for our team. As a marketing major, he was the team leader in advertising sales for our game program.

At the national tournament in Arizona that March, we edged Michigan-Dearborn 5–4 in the third-place game. However, the night that stands out from the late weeks of the season had occurred a few weeks earlier. Our home finale was a 5–3 win versus North Dakota State. We exploded for four third period goals, including one by Brian Wierson. Joe Schaffer scored twice during the game, and as the clock ran down, the crowd began to chant "MUR-DOCH, MUR-DOCH." It was my five hundredth win at Iowa State, an overwhelming moment to think of the hundreds of players and supporters who had helped us from the outdoor ice north of Beyer Hall to become one of the most popular teams on campus and consistent national championship contenders.

Bob Johnson had encouraged me to get involved with USA Hockey back when the organization was still known as the Amateur Hockey Association of the United States. As Bob watched what we were doing at Iowa State and other non-varsity programs, he was impressed that young players were staying active with the sport. When the ACHA was formed and I served as the organization's first president, I insisted our teams and players be registered with USA Hockey. Not many of the other schools were for it, but there were reasons the relationship was practical and advantageous.

On the financial side, the most relevant thing about being a member of USA Hockey is coverage under USA Hockey insurance. A large organization like that can get cheaper rates. I knew that from my connections with the insurance and investment industry. There have been times when smaller groups of schools have broken off for something different, like the AAU. Typically, they come back before long, because the players on their teams were brought up registering with USA Hockey each year.

In 1996, I was elected as a USA Hockey director, representing the ACHA. USA Hockey has two national meetings each year, with 1,200 or 1,500 people in various sessions sorting out issues in the sport. Much of the important work happens at the committee level. The adult council deals with teams and players who are eighteen and older, and that is an area where the ACHA has been a logical fit. Male and female, a large percentage of the adult players registered with USA Hockey are on ACHA teams.

Still, involvement isn't limited to one committee, and much of the crossover between councils makes sense. I've worked with the junior council and the officials' group, among others. On the junior council, they wanted to know where ACHA players were coming from, and of course, the answer, in large part, was junior teams. All tiers of junior hockey have young players who are looking for a quality education. As for officials, they would ask, "Does the ACHA do anything to train referees?" The answer: "Yes, we train officials with rules that are tweaked just slightly from USA Hockey's rulebook."

Taking an active role in USA Hockey created the chance to introduce our organization to the broader hockey community. More than once, I heard a variant of, "Well, that's just a club program, isn't it?"

"We don't refer to it as 'club' hockey," I would say over and over. "A club program is disorganized and lacks leadership. We don't. Most importantly, we're giving people the opportunity to play."

These were chances to educate and inform hockey leaders about forthcoming NCAA Division I programs like Arizona State and Penn State that were in the ACHA first. Building connections, both formal and informal, across all levels of the sport, I found that I could lobby to get things done. I've always been willing to talk to anybody, anywhere, and at any time. One of my aspirations was to create more opportunities for ACHA players to represent the United States in international competition. That became a reality as the 2000s began, and non-varsity schools were selected to stock the team that would go to the World University Games every other winter.

The ACHA had a second director position for many years. Hard as it may be to believe, for a long time, it was difficult to find a second person to serve. I was the director for fifteen or twenty years—even after retiring from coaching—and then suddenly, the director seat became more competitive. Other coaches saw that I was getting to be part of the World University Games and interacting with prestigious people in the sport. It had opened doors for me. I hope new directors stepping into their roles will be just as active and open to working with a broad group of people. Most importantly, I hope they will stand up for the ACHA and the important place it holds for players who might otherwise not have a place to play.

Although I am no longer an elected USA Hockey director, I am very pleased to still be active in the organization after receiving emeritus director status. It is a role that does not include a vote on issues, but I have the opportunity to offer suggestions and opinions and continue advocating for the over five hundred non-varsity college teams. During sessions over the past few years, I have been getting accustomed to this new role that is different from the Murdoch "you don't run to finish second philosophy." I've tried to cool my heels, but regardless, it is good to continue in service to an organization that has been so important to me and many others.

I was always getting campus "celebrities" to come to games or drop the ceremonial first puck. I enjoyed that, and I was fearless. So, one day, I called the university president's office. I invited President Martin Jischke to a hockey game. Some of the other adults around the hockey team reacted by saying, "Are you nuts? Wait until he sees the crowd and they're drinking beer."

I said to my wife, "Jane, we've got to make this as comfortable as possible."

I asked her to bring a blanket for the wooden bleachers where she would sit with the president and Mrs. Jischke, and sure enough, they were there that night. He arrived early enough that the students hadn't started to fill up the building yet. Our team was getting ready to go out for warm-ups, and I came up out of the locker room to visit with the president and his wife in the stands. There were three important questions that were part of the conversation. Dr. Jischke said to Jane, "Your husband's been around here for a while. How long has he been here?" Of course, Jane knew the exact year—twenty-five or thirty years, whatever it was at that point. He looked around at the steel building we had played in since 1980 and said, "This is quite a facility. Who owns this?" My wife said, "You do, Dr. Jischke."

"This is an Iowa State facility, really?"

By that point, students are starting to fill in and find their seats. All of them were wearing winter coats and had their gloves or mittens on. But they also had a beer in each hand as they walked by. It was a ten-cent beer night. President Jischke looked around and observed, "They're drinking *beer*."

Jane didn't hesitate and said, "You bet. Want my husband to get you a couple?"

He did, in fact, have a beer. Then, first thing you know, the students were saying, "That's the president of the university there." So, they were coming over to get pictures with him, and he would say, "Just a minute," and he'd set the beer down to the side so it wasn't in the picture. That was definitely one of the highlights of my career, and it proves I didn't always run afoul of administrators.

The end of the 1995–96 season was the first time we had made it back to the ACHA championship game since we won in 1992. Ohio University was the host and the defending champion. The school built its program fast and recruited hard, even landing some players who already had degrees from other schools. That eventually prompted an ACHA rule change requiring graduate students to have attended the same university where they were playing, so there would be more opportunity for undergrads to go to school and play hockey. Still, for a time, Ohio's average player age was twenty-four or twenty-five years old, while other schools' players were closer to nineteen or twenty. On the ice, Ohio did innovative things on special teams, and they had a lot of quality players from junior hockey leagues in Ontario.

There was some thought that Ohio could jump to Division I scholarship hockey. They had an NCAA program in the 1970s, but their facility made it impossible to transition back. I don't know if the building had seating for one thousand people. Our rivalry with Ohio was good at that point, because both of our teams were in the CSCHL. In the spring of 1996,

Ohio beat us in Ames for the CSCHL championship. That game finished 5–1, and a week later, they won by the same score during the national championship game at their small rink in Athens.

They got the better of us again at the 1997 championship hosted by Eastern Michigan. We had beaten Ohio during the regular season and went into the tournament as the top team after winning both the CSCHL regular season and playoff titles. The national final was a 1–1 game going to the third period. Ohio scored with eight minutes remaining and then held on for a 2–1 result. It was their third consecutive championship. We were runners-up for the fifth time in six championship appearances, despite having a program best 33–5–3 record.

Although Ohio won the title, we had the ACHA's best player in 1996–97. Doug Borud was not our highest scorer, but he did give us sixty points in forty games. At six feet, three inches tall and 230 pounds, he stood out any time he took the ice. We had been fortunate to bring him to Iowa State. He was from northern Minnesota, and during the 1992–93 season, Doug had played in the USHL for the Des Moines Buccaneers. Even though he was one of their oldest players, he only had about twenty regular season points but then got going in the playoffs. Doug scored a triple-overtime goal in one postseason game and then a couple more before Des Moines was eliminated. He also scored a half-dozen points at USA Hockey's National Junior Tournament. He was about a point-per-game player after the regular season ended but got only one college offer from Division III Wisconsin-Superior. After a semester there, Doug decided he liked Iowa better and came to Ames.

He had actually been our leading scorer in 1995–96. Doug's role was a little different in 1996–97, but he worked hard and showed a lot of leadership as one of our captains. I was very proud when he was recognized with the Bob Johnson Award that spring. Like Bill Ward before him, Doug went on to become an Iowa State assistant coach, and in fact, Bill and Doug were on staff together the next year.

The 1996–97 season had also been notable for the start of Iowa State's women's hockey team. I knew there were students from Minnesota and other states where girls would start off in youth hockey playing with the boys. Going to Iowa State and having the ability to continue in a women's program was a natural plus. There was interest among female students, and at the team's first meeting, over eighty attended. Women had already been involved in hockey intramurals for some time, and a few schools near us also had intramural teams, so those were ISU's early opponents. A few

A sunny day on campus with notable players of the '90s (*left to right*): Brian Wierson, Doug Borud and Rusty Crawford. *Bernie English*.

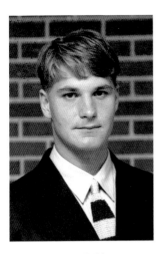

Rob Howitt made his way to Ames from northern Manitoba and was a workhorse goaltender for our program. *Author's collection.*

years later, the ACHA began offering women's hockey, and before long colleges were fielding teams in two women's divisions.

By 1997–98, Brian Wierson and Rusty Crawford were seniors, and we had a lineup that was heavy with upperclassmen. The team had been to consecutive ACHA championship games. We were missing some important players, but we were a strong team. Ames was also selected as the host site for the national tournament once again, so optimism was high that home ice might make the difference.

Senior goalie Rob Howitt was probably our most important individual player. As a junior, he had been in the net for twenty-eight of our thirty-three wins and was named our team MVP. Howitt had come from Thompson, Manitoba, which is even farther north than The Pas. He was six feet, two inches tall and fearless in the crease. His junior coach was Danny Nicholls, who had also come down from northern Manitoba to skate for me in the late 1980s. Danny had played a large role in getting Rob interested in Iowa State and vice versa. Rob won twenty-six more games in 1997–98 and gave the team back to back Bob Johnson Awards when the season was over.

Unfortunately, we could not ride Rob to the championship game. Instead, it was Penn State who ended Ohio's attempt to win four straight ACHA titles. Iowa State played in the third-place game against our CSCHL rivals from Illinois. Aside from being in conference and just across a state line, the Iowa State–Illinois rivalry was fed by that natural opposition between Big Ten and Big XII universities. Illinois has a big rink that's wider than normal, because they use it for speed skating. When we would go to Champaign, the fans would sell out the building every night and would dump coffee over the railing onto our players and the coaches, so there was a lot of hostility between the programs.

In this case, we were on home ice. Illinois took an early lead, but we came back and scored five straight goals. By the start of the third period, it was a one-goal game again, and I used the same tactic that had helped us win the national championship in 1992. Rob Howitt was getting worn down, so I brought in our backup goalie, Mike Grammatikos, who was also a senior. He played great down the stretch, and we added a couple of insurance goals to win, 7–4. It was our thirty-fourth win that season, a new record. All of those players, and especially the seniors, had such high hopes to win the championship at home after two close calls. Even though it didn't happen, it was great that they had the chance to win their last game together.

10

WINNING, THEN LOSING

air or not, as it's told today, the story of Iowa State's 1998–99 season centers on Darcy and Darren Anderson. The Andersons were from North Bay, Ontario, and had come to Ames together in 1994 after playing junior hockey at Niagara Falls. I had first met them at a hockey camp I was holding in eastern Ontario. Darren was a year or two older and an exceptional student, as well as a good hockey player and team leader. Darcy didn't get along quite so easily with the other players on our team. He was self-confident to the point that he seemed to have all the answers, but there's no doubt he was very talented and an exceptional scorer.

Both brothers were a little over six feet tall and solidly built. Even though they were each larger than average, they were very protective of each other. It wasn't long before I stopped playing them on the same line. If one of them was hit by an opponent—whether the play was clean or not—the other would retaliate and take a penalty. It certainly saved us some penalty minutes and probably made us a better team to have them playing with different line combinations.

Near the end of their first year, they got a telephone call from North Bay. A serious family situation had developed, and they needed to go home right away to be there for their parents. I won't go into the details, but it was truly a life-or-death situation in their immediate family. Both boys returned to Ontario and did not make it back to Iowa State until the fall semester of 1996. In the winter of 1996–97, Darcy led the team with one hundred points, and Darren had fifty-one goals. Even with all the success he was having with our program, Darcy was looking for something else, and he was gone again in the fall of 1997.

Initially, he wanted to play professional hockey. He spent some time with a team in Michigan, where he had a cousin or uncle who was coaching. As I understood it, he skated for a couple of weeks and might have played in some exhibition games for that team in the Colonial Hockey League. It wasn't working out there, so Darcy applied to go to Denver University to play for the Pioneers. The Denver hockey program looked over his record and said, "Well, you played for Iowa State. Have you played any pro hockey?"

"Well, not really. My cousin is coaching in the Colonial Hockey League, and I practiced with him for a while."

Denver apparently checked it out. They believed he could play and got it cleared by the NCAA that he could be eligible. Meanwhile, Darren had been elected as one of our captains. He was having a great season in 1997–98. Ultimately, he was our top goal scorer again, and he led the team with seventy-three points. As the first semester continued, Darren came to me and said, "Hey, even though my brother Darcy was looking at a couple of other options, I don't think it's going to work out. I'll get him here by Christmas."

Darcy came back to play in the second semester, and he went right into the lineup. I made the mistake of thinking, "Well, he's eligible at Denver University; he'll be eligible at Iowa State," without clearing it with the ACHA's administrative board. Darcy did help us that year. He didn't quite play in half of our games, but he had ten goals and thirteen assists. On a team with a lot of weapons, he was one of many good players. When we finished third during the ACHA tournament in Ames, no one questioned Darcy's contributions to our season.

Back for the fall of 1998, Darren and Darcy were both seniors. They were every bit as good as you would hope for them to be with the experience and success they had up until then. Darcy led us with fifty-seven goals and 103 points. Darren was not far behind with thirty-four goals and forty-four assists. Between them, they scored twenty-two power play goals, and while our power play was good, we were even more dominant at even strength, outscoring other teams by more than a 3–1 ratio. We shattered the Iowa State record from a year before and won thirty-seven games, including the very last game during the ACHA championships hosted by the University of Delaware.

Although hindsight might bring Darcy and Darren Anderson to mind first, Iowa State made it to the top of the ACHA in 1998–99 thanks to the efforts of a lot of other players. After Rob Howitt's graduation, we had a pair of underclassmen in goal. Nick Makris had played high school hockey in suburban Chicago and then saw a little time as an Iowa State backup in 1997–98. Dan LaVoie was a freshman from northern Ontario and was just five feet, nine inches tall but very sharp. Dan played a little more, but the load was more balanced than it had been in the preceding years. When you have two goalies who can push each other, that usually means you get the best from both of them.

On the blue line, Greg Jones was our anchor and was eventually voted the team's outstanding defensive player. Greg was originally from Des Moines but had played for a couple of years at NCAA Division III St. Mary's in Winona, Minnesota. He was reliable in his own end but also added offense and was our leading defensive scorer with fifty-one points. A couple of freshmen from Canada also stood out. Rob Rose was from Newfoundland and brought as much size as anyone on defense. He also added experience from a couple of Junior "A" seasons in Ontario. Marc Sarazin was the other standout Canadian. His background included several junior years in Ontario, too, and as a result, he was a little older than the typical freshman.

Among the forwards, Mike Anderson was not related to Darren or Darcy. Mike was from Clear Lake, Iowa, and was a junior by the fall of 1998. He really showed a lot of improvement from year to year, growing into his six-foot-three-inch-tall frame. Mike was always physical and became an important leader; he would be one of our captains the next year. Jesse Monell was another in-state recruit; he had started playing youth hockey in Sioux City, moved up to the high school team and eventually played three seasons in the USHL with the Sioux City Musketeers. As a twenty-year-old, Jesse was among the Musketeers' top scorers, which is a real accomplishment for a hometown kid in that league. Brian Paolello was a junior forward who would become an Iowa State captain for the 1999–2000 season. Brian had been a star high school player in Illinois, while his older brother, John, was playing for me in Ames. He didn't have overwhelming size, but he played with an edge and made the game difficult for opposing players. Brian was one we lost too soon; in 2017, he died in his early forties.

The fall of 1998 was the beginning of one of the best careers in Iowa State hockey history. Glenn Detulleo was from Ontario but had gone east to play junior hockey in the Maritime provinces. French was his first language, but he was an exceptional student. On the ice, he set ISU records that still stand. Glenn had the same desire I had to win at every aspect of the game. He was an exceptional skater, puck handler and shooter. He wasn't a big guy—only five feet, seven inches tall—but he played with a lot of heart. In a different era, as the game opened up and speed became increasingly important relative to size, who knows how far he could have gone in professional hockey.

As it was, he still had a long professional career. He played in a couple of European leagues and then with several teams in the North American minor leagues. The last place he was playing was Huntsville, Alabama, in the Southern Professional Hockey League, where he was having a pretty good season. One Friday night, he was a leading scorer for the team, and on Saturday, the owner came around and said, "Now, you're head coach." He has been there ever since and probably could have moved up and been coaching at a higher level than Huntsville. I would guess that the owner was sharp enough to know Glenn had learned a few things. The team draws sellout crowds and has won a couple of SPHL championships, so maybe he has found that Huntsville is for him what Ames has been for me.

As a freshman in 1998–99, Glenn was second only to Darcy Anderson in scoring. He had eighty-six points in forty games. He almost scored forty goals. Only Marc Sarazin's plus/minus was better (+64 to +60). Like I said, that was just the beginning. Over his three years at Iowa State, Glenn led the ACHA in scoring twice. He finished with over three hundred points and won the Bob Johnson Award in 2001. He was an asset to the Ames community and helped raise money for charitable causes. And even while he was doing all of that, Glenn still graduated ahead of schedule, thanks in part to some college credits he had earned while playing junior hockey. Glenn Detulleo might be the best example of a player who made the most of the opportunities offered to him by the ACHA.

As good as Iowa State had been in the 1990s, the 1998–99 team was on another level. We won the CSCHL regular season and then the conference postseason tournament. We were the top team in the ACHA going into nationals, and our 33–4 mark was already on the verge of tying the record we had set the year before. The championships were hosted by the University of Delaware during the first week of March. Their rink was about ten years old and located right on campus. With 2,500 seats, it was a little bigger than a typical ACHA building, and the tournament was held on their wider Olympic-sized ice.

We started out by beating Eastern Michigan 7–2. They had played the night before, because there were ten teams that qualified. The bottom four teams played single-elimination games to get into the round robin stage. In our second game, we beat Delaware 7–1 for our record thirty-fifth win. However, since Delaware was the host, that game was held at seven o'clock. We had to come back the next afternoon to play at 1:00 p.m. against an Ohio University team that had a full twenty-four hours to recover.

Even though this was pool play, it was really an elimination game, because both teams were 2–0 in the tournament, so the winner would go on to the championship game. Ohio scored early in the first period. They thought they had made it 2–0 a few minutes later, but their second goal was disallowed because the puck had been batted in. The game was tied by the second intermission, and the score was still 1–1 as the third period was coming to a close. Jesse Monell got the puck near our blue line and made it up the ice. It really opened up for him; suddenly, he was on a breakaway, and he scored to make it a 2–1 game, which ended up being the final score. There are a lot of people who say one of our other players was offside, but the video was inconclusive.

The win put us past the opponent that had beaten us in the 1996 and 1997 finals. The championship game pitted us against Penn State. When we'd lost to them during the 1998 tournament in Ames, it cost us the chance to play for the championship at home. However, by January 1999, we had already played and won a rematch against Penn State during a tournament in their building. That win, the game tape, and the scouting we did in Delaware gave us a plan: shoot high toward their goalie's blocker arm. That was where we were going to beat him.

In fact, both goalies' shoulders were part of the story that night. Dan LaVoie had an injury that he brought with him from junior hockey: a shoulder that was prone to dislocating. It happened in the first period of the championship game. In most cases, the trainers would say, "He's done. He can't play anymore," but I'd learned a trick of the trade. I told Dan to grab the center of his jersey, just a little above the belt, and shrug. The dislocation would pop back into place 99 percent of the time, and in his case, it did.

Then in the second period, he said, "Coach, it's out again. Hurts like hell."

But he did the shrug, and it went back in.

Near the start of the third period, he said, "It's out again. Damn shoulder."

For a few months, Iowa State hockey had possession of the Murdoch Cup, but today, that championship is "vacated." *Bernie English.*

This time, it didn't pop right back in. He went to the door jam and hit his shoulder on it trying to relocate it himself. I got him to calm down. We did the shrug again, and it came around. I think Penn State knew that he was hurting, and they were crashing the net, trying to get him out of the game. Dan hung in there, and our players protected him. It helped that we put almost fifty shots on goal at the other net.

Tom Grimwood had scored on the first or second shift of the game, high to the blocker side. They tied the score near the end of the period. Mike Anderson tipped a shot in the second period to give us a lead, and Penn State tied it again. Then we had a 3–2 lead thanks to Jesse Monell, but that score didn't quite make it to intermission, so it was 3–3 going to the third. Finally, we were able to follow up one goal with another; Mike Ogbourne and Mike Anderson each scored in the first couple of minutes after intermission. Grimwood added another goal, and the game finished 6–4. Darcy and Darren Anderson were on the all-tournament team, although neither of them scored in the championship game. Greg Jones, Dan LaVoie, and Jesse Monell were also recognized. We celebrated, and it was a great moment. I took a lot of kidding about finally winning the Murdoch Cup, which had been renamed a year or two after we'd won in 1992. Unfortunately, we only got to keep the trophy with my name on it for a couple of months.

In April 1999, someone called the ACHA with a "tip" about Darcy Anderson. That sparked an investigation and review that lasted for months. I was optimistic at first. I assumed that because Denver University had declared Darcy was eligible there, he was eligible at Iowa State. I left it at that. The ACHA chose to approach it a differently; their view was that if he practiced and played a couple of exhibition games with a minor league team, he was ineligible. By June, they were ready to retract the national championship.

I fought it for several weeks, but the situation reached a point where everything stacked against us. All of a sudden, Iowa State vice-presidents were calling me into their offices, saying, "What are you doing? Are you playing ineligible players, or what's going on?"

I said, "No, here's the reason I believe he's eligible, and I think we've got a good case. Denver University, a Division I NCAA team, declared him eligible if he'd enrolled there, and they reviewed all the background information."

There was no support. The response was, "Well, Denver University is NCAA, and you're in the ACHA. The ACHA calls the shots. You back off; we don't need any controversy, and we don't need lawyers crawling all over the place. It's a done deal, so back off, or we're going to fire your ass."

I don't think I'll ever know all the details about that anonymous tip. If Michigan-Dearborn had beaten Penn State and had been our opponent in the final, would this have ever come up? I'll never know that either. I won't know what would have happened if USA Hockey or lawyers or truly independent investigators had looked into the situation, although I think Iowa State probably would have fired me for fighting it. The thing I do know is that the administration wouldn't throw its full support behind a team they considered to be just a "club."

So, I backed off. We lost the national championship that we had won. A lot of the guys had already purchased national championship rings or done other things to commemorate our win. I still feel bad about that. By then, it was summertime, and our players were gone. Fortunately, there was a lot to do to prepare for the fall—selling tickets and advertising. And I could say, "We'll just win another one," and focus on getting ready for the next season. Still, it stings me just a little bit whenever the ACHA puts out information and notes "vacated" for 1999.

Our players and the people who cared about the program were certainly still thinking about what happened as we got ready for the new season. It was right there on the cover of our game program: "Don't get mad…GET

EVEN!" Inside, Brian Paolello wrote about the prior season in the preview for the year ahead. As he put it, "the Cyclone team was practically a shoe-in to win the crown. The allegations that spread of an illegal player was an easy explanation as to why few teams could compete with [us]."

We didn't "just win another one," as we all hoped, but we did get even to a degree. Penn State came to Ames just after Christmas break in January 2000. Although they won the first game and were ahead going into the third on Saturday, we came back. Glenn Detulleo had a hat trick, and we scored four times in the third period to win 5–3. For a lot of our players and fans, it was the most important of our thirty-two wins that year.

II

THIS IS BIGGER THAN THEY TOLD ME

The World University Games began a few years after World War II. Like the Olympics, there are competitions for both summer and winter sports, although the events are held every two years instead of every four. In the late 1980s, USA Hockey entered a team but was not involved during many of the years that followed. Before he died, Bob Johnson gave me a brief introduction. He said, "You need to coach a team going to the World University Games. Teams from different countries get together, and you have a little tournament."

Of course, I got in a habit with Bob Johnson; whatever he suggested, I was willing to do. Several years passed, and nothing happened until I was at a USA Hockey conference almost a decade later. Art Berglund was responsible for many of the U.S. teams that went to different events. He and a few others said, "Al, we've got to talk to you." And they pulled me out of a meeting, out into the hallway to say, "We'd like you to take a team to the World University Games. Would you be interested in doing that? You've been taking teams internationally to China and Australia, Russia—all over the world."

They thought my experience would be valuable, and I thought, "Well, another international trip wouldn't hurt."

However, that was only a few months before the 1999 event. There was no turnaround time for player evaluation, selection, training, and all the things that are required to build a team. Instead, we decided to aim for 2001 in Zakopane, Poland. I wanted the United States to be represented by an

ACHA all-star team, and there was some pushback at first. It was suggested we get an NCAA goaltender or some other NCAA players for more depth.

I said, "Well, it's just a small tournament. What's the big deal? I'd like to bring exposure to the ACHA."

Ultimately, they agreed to let me take a team that was completely made up of ACHA players. I didn't know it—maybe Bob Johnson and Art Berglund didn't either—but it was a bigger event than they had indicated. The eligibility rules were also much different than what we think of for college sports in the United States. The first time we went, I think the age limit was twenty-eight. Canada brought retired professional players who were going to school after their careers had ended. The Canadian roster had twenty-six- and twenty-seven-year-old guys with a lot of experience. As a result, Canada tended to be one of the stronger contenders, along with Russia and other nations from Europe.

In preparation, I had gone to the U.S. Olympic Committee offices and said, "I've had good luck at Iowa State finding sponsorships so we can get a trip like this paid for. We don't want each of the players having to pay their full way. I can sell advertising."

They said, "Who are you thinking about selling to?"

Years of fundraising, like this Iowa State call-a-thon, gave me tools to help our 2001 World University Games team get to Poland. *Bernie English.*

"Well, we've got to get over there on an airline, you know, so if we can't get a full sponsorship package from United Airlines, there's probably an airline that'll do it."

The guy from the USOC shook his head. "No, we've already got the airlines wrapped up."

"Well, I've had good luck selling hotels, and wherever we stay over there, there's got to be a way we can get some of the rooms for free on a trade."

"No, we've got all the hotels wrapped up where we stay all around the world."

"How about restaurants? Food?"

Same thing.

I was backed into a corner, but once we had our team, I managed to teach the players how to get sponsorships from their hometowns and areas around the colleges where they played. We made it work. None of that shows up in the box score, but it was a huge part of getting to the World University Games in February 2001.

Initially, there was a process for ACHA programs to nominate their players to be on this U.S. National University Team. Then a panel of eight coaches decided who would go. In later years, players could fill out an application form, and USA Hockey would hold a summer tryout camp with seventy-five or one hundred players signed up to be evaluated. In 2001, Brian Wilkie from Minot State and Chad Cassel from Illinois were my assistant coaches. Shawn Bergstrand was our top goalie. He had been offered a full scholarship at the University of North Dakota, but for one reason or another, he went to Minot State instead. Jack Pepper from Ohio University was chosen as our captain. To this day, I still hear from him, and he talks about how wonderful that team was. We had players from all the top ACHA schools: Penn State, Kent State, Michigan-Dearborn. Six of the twenty-two players were from Iowa State. They knew my philosophy: you play hard, you play to win no matter who you're playing against, and there's nobody in the world who should overawe you.

Fortunately, I observed the lesson I had learned about international trips so many years earlier: you make the trip yourself the summer before. At that time, my son Sean was working in Luxembourg. The plan was to go see him and then go to Poland for an advance look at the venue and its surroundings.

However, I was still using my Canadian passport. My wife, Jane, had an American passport. At the Polish border, they were ready to let her in with no problem, but they wouldn't let me in.

When we made it back home, I said, "I've got to get this changed."

I made some calls, and the prevailing advice was to contact Senator Chuck Grassley's office. I explained the situation and said that I had been at Iowa State since 1969. I never met Senator Grassley personally, but his administrative assistant took care of everything in just over a week. I had all the paperwork and everything done for American citizenship after thirty years of living in Ames.

Although this was a USA Hockey trip, the principle of making it an educational experience did not change. After arriving, we spent a day bussing north from Zakopane to Krakow, and then west to the Auschwitz Concentration Camp. The camps have been maintained to look as they did during World War II, and we heard the terrible stories of life and death there. It turned out that two of the players on our U.S. team had Jewish backgrounds. It should be no surprise that it was a hard day, draining and disturbing. But I think with perspective, those players today would tell you they are glad that I had them make that trip.

Also unforgettable—in a completely different way—were the opening ceremonies.

The organizers or someone from the USOC asked, "Do you want to go?"

I said, "What do we do there?"

"Well, you walk in and see other athletes."

"Why not?" You know I was always one to say, "Yeah, let's try this."

We went over, and they held the ceremony at the base of the big mountain where the ski competitions were to be conducted during the games. People were skiing down the slope with lights. Horses were trotting in, pulling sleighs. It was a big event. That's when I started to get nervous; this was bigger than Bob Johnson and Art Berglund had told me. It turns out that the World University Games are the largest sporting event anywhere, except for the Olympics. Fifty or sixty different countries are represented during the winter competition, and it's right up there when it comes to the number of participants and the number of fans.

That was the start of it. I was hooked.

Ukraine was our first opponent when the competition began. They waxed us pretty well. I got the feeling toward the end of the game that they were holding off so they wouldn't get into double figures and really embarrass us. That game ended 9–1. From the bench, I had seen the Russian coaches watching from the front row and taking notes throughout the first period. Then I saw them get up and leave. They must have figured, "These Americans are terrible. They're just young kids."

That was to my advantage. I liked that they got up and left. Russia had enjoyed a lot of success at the World University Games, and they were our next opponent. My players had a great practice on the day in between the two games. I gathered them around before practice began and said, "OK, we're going to do something different. I know the style of play that the Russians have at full strength. I know the style of play for their penalty killing. I know their style of play on their power play. We're going to beat them at every aspect, because we're going to be unorthodox."

I call their style the Russian weave—they would never stay in their lanes. As a matter of fact, by the time they got into the offensive zone, they were playing off wing. Left-handed shots were playing right wing going into the offensive zone, whether they started there or not. It didn't matter because they could catch passes on their backhand. I had learned all that from those summer trips to Russia in the 1970s and playing and watching them in the years since. They also had the habit of going behind the opposing net and creating offense from there. To chase the guy behind the net wasn't a good system, but we made it work, because they weren't expecting it. I also told our players, "Don't be afraid to get physical, because the referees aren't expecting it either, and they won't call a penalty on a guy they weren't expecting to go back there."

Like magic, it worked.

The game was scoreless after the first period, but then the Russians went ahead in the middle of the second. It was getting close to intermission when they went on a power play, and sure enough, they set up behind our net and sent their other players swooping in circles around the ice.

"Don't chase those guys," I thought to myself on the bench. "Hit the guy behind the net."

Sure enough, their forward behind our goal was watching his own players and *smack*, our guy knocked him flat on his butt, stole the puck, and fed it up the ice to a teammate for a breakaway shorthanded goal. The Russians were looking at me as if to say, "You can't do that. You can't play that way."

We scored again in the last minute of the second period and were ahead 2–1.

Shawn Bergstrand seemed to play really well for two periods, and then he would fall apart in the third. It's like he would leave it all on the ice for the first forty minutes and wouldn't have anything left. I used some psychology there. At intermission, I was motivating our players, telling them, "We're a third-period team." And I'd go over to Shawn and say, "OK, we got to get this second period out of the way. The second period is coming up. You always play great in the second period." He had to be thinking, "Haven't we already played the second period?" But I kept emphasizing it with him quietly on the side: it was the *second* period coming up.

Shawn had an outstanding third period.

We scored a couple more goals, and then, all of a sudden, you could just feel the Russians coming back. I shortened the bench and shortened the shifts quite a bit. There were times that we had only twenty or thirty seconds between line changes. They got one goal back. They were circling and swarming all over our zone. I told the team, "You've got to play them out at the top of the circles. Don't let them get inside for rebounds or tip ins. This is no problem. We're the better team. You guys have all kinds of energy left."

That's what I told them, but as I looked down the bench, our team was absolutely drained. I was buying time on line changes. The referees would come over and say, "Coach, you've got to be quicker on the line changes."

I said, "Well, I'm not sure who I'm putting on yet."

I knew who I was putting on.

I played our better players a lot. I had one big defenseman who was very good. Unfortunately, he was so big, he got penalties for elbowing or roughing just because he was so much taller than everybody. I couldn't take a chance on him playing much. Nat Little was one of the Iowa State players on the trip, and every other shift that this big defenseman was supposed to be out there, I sent out Nat Little. Here we were, protecting a late lead with four forwards on the ice, and the Russians were a little stymied: "How can you do that?"

We were a team full of believers, and we weren't the only ones. The crowd in the stands—three thousand or four thousand Polish fans—for the last minute or minute and a half of the game began chanting, "U-S-A, U-S-A."

Holy crap. Who would ever think this? It was like the Olympics.

When the horn sounded at the end of the game, they poured on the ice. People were hugging me. One guy, a big guy in a big fur coat, came up and said, "This is wonderful for USA. You did so well." I remember that hug to this day.

After the game, I didn't say anything about training rules. That was a way to let the players know they could enjoy the win and celebrate a little. The next day would be an off day. Back at the hotel, a celebratory beer couldn't have tasted better. It was one of the most wonderful moments of my life and the best game I've ever been a part of.

Just like being the first president of the ACHA and staying in that role for only a couple of years, it was important to me that other people had the chance to coach during the World University Games. Still, I was fortunate that USA Hockey kept asking me to come back as a general manager or with other titles as part of the U.S. National University Team. Since the event is held every two years, it occupied a lot of time, and I wasn't able to take the Iowa State team overseas. We made it to Canada and Alaska and other interesting places but not back to Europe or Asia. Still, I'm happy to say that a lot of Iowa State players had the chance to represent their country at the World University Games.

I think having this international recognition was important to the ACHA. USA Hockey could have insisted on a Division I goalie on a full scholarship or some NCAA players at other positions, but they didn't. It was all ACHA players. As a result, all of these athletes came back and told their teammates and friends, "Oh, God, you wouldn't believe it. The flight, the international food, beating the Russians! Holy cow!" The ACHA grew quickly during those years, and I think having the opportunity to play at an international level was one of the factors.

Joe Battista from Penn State was the head coach and I was the general manager in 2003. The United States didn't win a game, but we were close in all the games. Joe's team played well and was very organized. I talked to him a lot about what we did with the Russians and about how sometimes you have to be unorthodox. Chad Cassel was another good coach from Illinois in 2005 and 2007. As general manager, I wasn't afraid to speak my mind when things weren't going well and was probably more outspoken and assertive than most general managers.

At one point, I said, "Chad, when you played against Iowa State, your guys played harder than you're playing right now. What's going on? This is the opportunity of a lifetime."

He might not have liked what I was saying, but if pushing those buttons and making him think, "I'll show you, Al," got him to sit a guy who wasn't playing hard, it was worth it. I think the coaches would tell you, in hindsight, those moments helped make our teams more competitive. In the years I was general manager, coaches had the freedom to do what they wanted with my support. They didn't necessarily agree with everything I said, and I didn't agree with everything they did, but at the same time, I believe I was doing all I could to elevate them to a higher level.

The games brought me back to a couple of places I had been with Iowa State teams years before. In 2005, we were in Innsbruck. Then four years later, Harbin was the host. Austria had changed less from my first trip; China was much different than it had been in 1991. The 2007 World University Games were held in Torino, Italy, not long after the Winter Olympics had been there. Our teams have gone to Turkey, Spain, and Kazakhstan. Yet wherever we go around the world, USA Hockey makes it a first-class experience for our players with travel, accommodations, and equipment that make us feel like the whole country is behind us. The support staff and equipment managers always make us look like a million bucks whenever we step out on the ice in those USA jerseys.

12

ONWARD AND UPWARD

Offseason hockey camps in Ames provided some additional revenue for our rink and drew attention to Iowa State hockey among young players from the region. I'd hold camps for kids for four to six weeks in the summer, so ice stayed in that building twelve months a year. Eventually, a hump developed in the middle of the ice. There was frost going down ten or twelve feet in the ground, causing the surface to swell. The center of the ice became crowned like a football field, so you could be playing left wing and not be able to see where the puck was going on a pass to the right wing.

Some of the hose clamps that kept the piping connected were starting to break. That was a more serious problem, because it meant ammonia coolant could escape. Although the facility was owned by the university, it was managed and operated by the City of Ames. Nancy Carroll was the director of parks and recreation; she came in at one point and said, "There's a leak somewhere. We've got to shut the facility down. It could be dangerous to people."

She was surprised and not very happy when she saw how arena manager Wayne Kitchingman and I were approaching the problem. We got a pickaxe and went digging through the boarding at one end. Fortunately, we found the hose clamp that was broken pretty quickly. We fixed it without any problems, and we were lucky because ammonia really can be dangerous. That got us by, but it was clear that this rink, where we had played for almost twenty years, did not have many years left.

As early as the mid-1990s, we started to plan for a new building. My goal was a facility that would seat at least five thousand people, because that was the unwritten rule for consideration as an NCAA Division I program. The old Cyclone Area Community Center had been built with volunteer labor and small donations. The new facility seemed headed the same direction, but Iowa State students got behind our cause. Student government committed to almost $2 million from student fees for the new facility. So, I went to university officials and said, "Hey, the students are ready to give $2 million. Will the university match that?"

Their suggestion was to get funding from the City of Ames. Little did I know, the city had a reputation of not donating one penny of tax money to anything associated with the university or university programs. They viewed those things as the school's responsibility. Still, between the university president's office and the Ames City Council, a referendum was scheduled for a $2 million bond issue to match the students' contribution.

To pass a bond referendum, you need 60 percent of the people to vote in favor. How would we get a supermajority when a bond issue had never been passed in Ames to support a university-owned facility? Well, there was Murdoch, the salesman. During the middle of the season, I went on a six-week campaign—all of January, plus the first two weeks of February—giving presentations every night. I spoke to every service organization, every community club, every residence hall floor, all the fraternities and all the sororities, building an army of people who said, "Hey, this is a good deal. We can play broomball until two or three in the morning." The local residents' groups said, "Hey, this will give us an opportunity for our kids or become an amenity that makes Ames attractive over other communities."

In those six weeks, I gave 167 public presentations. I remember one night in particular at the Towers Residence Hall, which was nearest to the rink. I was giving presentations floor by floor, when it got to be eleven o'clock or midnight. I found myself talking about this vote to three guys who were sitting on the floor, drunk because they had just left the bars. Still, I gave the presentation, and at the end, they said, "We'll vote for that, Coach Murdoch."

It absolutely exhausted me, but at the same time, I knew it was for a good cause.

Sure enough, we got 83 percent of the vote. I thought, "We're going Division I now. We'll build a new facility, and we'll have five thousand seats. It will finally happen."

That hope only lasted until a meeting I had with a group of ISU administrators and city officials. I went into it feeling like we were going to have the best facility in the country. Then, at one point, a hand went up from

The piping is in place and awaiting the concrete floor in this construction photograph from Ames/ISU Ice Arena. *Bernie English.*

one of these smartass, know-it-all administrators, "Coach Murdoch, why didn't you ask for more money? Eighty-three percent voted in favor, so you could have gotten more."

I thought, "You jerks."

None of those people had gone out to give presentations. There still wasn't genuine support from the powers that be. The sentiment was, "You got money to put in ice, and after that, you can put in as much seating as you can get."

It turned out I wasn't done fundraising yet. We built a professional-style locker room. Anyone who donated $1,000 got their name placed on a locker stall. There were twenty-two or twenty-four alums and businesses who stepped up, and to this day, it still looks as good as any locker room in any NCAA building. There are about 1,100 seats above that locker room on the south side of the rink, looking across at the team benches and Iowa State's championship banners. The Ames/ISU Ice Arena opened in 2001.

At the same time I was selling Iowa State hockey to voters in Ames, Glenn Detulleo was selling it to fans from the ice. I could put any linemates with him, and he would make those teammates better. Everyone liked playing with him; they didn't know how he got the puck to their sticks so accurately while two opponents were holding him or cross-checking him. Without being told, Glenn would have a bucket of pucks out on a tennis court in the summertime, shooting pucks at a target from a slick sheet of plastic. He was always in exceptional condition. After a particularly tough game, he walked through the locker room with his shirt off. There were welts and bruises all over him from where the other team had tried to slow him down, but he never really showed pain.

Opponents had to respect him all the time. Of course, he was dangerous on the power play, but I also used him for penalty killing, because he was so smart. During one game against a school from Wisconsin, they had one or two players who would shadow Glenn whenever he was on the ice, regardless of the situation. It was one of the funniest experiences I ever had: they were on a power play and we were playing a man short, yet they were still shadowing *him*. He was that good.

We were a young team in 1999–2000, but Glenn still had over one hundred points, and we came up just short of the ACHA Final Four. Each season, our first goal was to move into the top ten or twelve teams in the country, whatever the number was to qualify for the tournament. Our second goal was to move into the top four. Goal number three: don't be fourth, get an even better seed. We were pretty good at taking those steps and raising our level of play. In the 2001 tournament, we were the fifth seed. We came back from the tournament in Arizona with a third-place finish after losing to Delaware in the semifinals but then beating Illinois in the consolation game.

Glenn had 122 points and became the fourth Cyclone to win the Bob Johnson Award as the ACHA's top player. The two of us went to the Hobey Baker dinner, and Glenn was recognized with a round of applause. That was the year the great Michigan State goalie Ryan Miller won the Hobey Baker Trophy. Ron Mason, my old friend from the Soviet coaching exchange in the 1970s, was the head coach at Michigan State. Ron, Glenn, Ryan Miller, and I all had our picture taken together to celebrate that great night.

Glenn Detulleo was the most gifted player at Iowa State during that time, but there was another forward whose choice to join our program was even more gratifying to me. My son Andrew had played a year of junior hockey in Sweden but broke his arm during a tryout with the Des Moines Buccaneers. That meant he was out of luck for the USHL at that point, but when his

At the Hobey Baker presentation with (*left to right*) Glenn Detulleo, Hobey Baker–winner Ryan Miller and Ron Mason. *Author's collection.*

arm healed, he played in another junior league out west. We've got relatives in Dauphin, Manitoba, and that's where Andrew played the following year. He had a great season. When he got back, he visited a few colleges. One day, he came into my office and said, "Well, I made a decision to play for an outstanding program with an outstanding coach."

I said, "Oh, Wisconsin? Notre Dame? Brown?"

"No, Iowa State."

Well, holy cow.

He ended up playing four years for me starting in the fall of 1999 and was a captain his senior year. I'm sure I don't even know half the story of playing as the coach's son. It was probably a hell of a lot tougher on him than it was on me, especially in those first years when I made decisions the other players didn't like. Iowa State made it back to the ACHA final four in 2002, when he was a junior. He was our leading scorer with fifty points as a senior, and he played in the World University Games twice. Now, Andrew is coaching his own son at the youth level in the Ames/ISU Ice Arena.

Iowa State hockey had a new rink and was continuing to be successful in the ACHA. At the same time, the team's relationship with some administrators was deteriorating. They insisted that we refer to ourselves as the "Iowa State Hockey *Club*." One year, they had us repeatedly insert a disclaimer in our game program: "An Officially Registered Student Organization, ISU Men's Ice Hockey is a non-varsity sport and not affiliated with the ISU Department of Athletics or the NCAA." They wanted us to act like other campus clubs. For whatever reason, our professionalism, our success, our notoriety was a threat.

The low point came in the 2004–05 season. We were pushing the envelope, playing well, getting media coverage. That rankled the dean of students' office and the vice-president for student affairs' office. The message was: "You guys have no choice. You better start acting like a club." And they just kept pushing us and pushing us until our players and supporters snapped back.

Rod French had been a huge backer since the beginning of Iowa State hockey. He and his wife, Connie, were in Des Moines and owned the largest Kenworth semitruck dealership in the world at that time. They had connections with people at the university and were major boosters for the athletics department, as well as other programs on campus. Rod was in a position to say to President Gregory Geoffroy, "Murdoch and the hockey team are being harassed by your administrators. Why do you condone that?"

That led to a meeting. It was after a Sunday afternoon men's basketball game, so nobody could be there until the basketball game was over well into the evening. President Geoffroy was sitting at the head of the conference table in Beardshear Hall. To his right was the entire group of administrators we'd been wrangling with, down to the residence hall director, who hated that we put up hockey flyers on the walls in the residence halls. On my side of the table, there was Rod French, along with David Moline and Scott Hagen, who were both seniors and had played in the World University Games that winter. David Moline's father was there and so was an attorney he had brought along.

The meeting started out with the administrators' grievances: "They put up flyers when they're not supposed to, so we told them quit or they're going to be suspended." That went on for a half hour or forty-five minutes—picky little stuff.

David Moline's dad was a very successful businessman, and finally, he'd heard enough and spoke up, saying, "President Geoffroy, I don't understand how you can allow undergraduate students at your university to be harassed like this."

It was quiet in the room, and one of the administrators eventually responded, "It's not really harassment, it's just following the rules." So, it was clear that neither side was hearing the other. Ultimately, it came down to the hockey team being answerable to a department we could work with.

The president pointed out, "The dean of students has been the one overseeing the program."

I said, "No, it doesn't fit there."

"Well, maybe the office of student affairs?"

"No, it doesn't fit there either."

We were starting to run out of people

President Geoffroy eventually said to me, "Dr. Murdoch, where do you think it should report?"

Again, the room was just silent.

I said, "The vice-president for business and finance, Warren Madden, is a fair person and an intelligent person."

"Warren, will you do that?" President Geoffroy asked.

Warren Madden could hardly say no, and it was an arrangement that worked very well for many years after that. Rod French was always there for us behind the scenes. In tight years, his support helped us avoid cuts in the hockey program until we could fundraise to cover the gap. From that point forward, we really operated like a varsity program in all aspects of what we did.

After Glenn Detulleo, the first decade of the 2000s was not as high-scoring. I wanted Iowa State players to know how to play defense and how to shut down the opposing team. When we didn't have the puck, we had systems for defense, and I think we got fairly good at them. We had to be a good penalty killing team due to our rough, physical style. Opposing teams had a fair number of power plays, but we didn't give them too many power play goals.

Even in higher-scoring years, there was a thought that if you came to play for Al Murdoch, you better know how to play defense. I think it was attractive for defensemen and defensive forwards; they could have opportunities to score within our system, but you had to play defense first. We played an aggressive forechecking system. You could have a zero forecheck or a one-man forecheck or a two-man forecheck. My tendency was to play a two-man forecheck: the first guy plays the body, and the second guy gets the puck and a scoring opportunity. For opponents that were quicker and better at moving the puck, it might have been a one-man or zero forecheck, but then you better have the open players covered.

One of our best defensive players around this time was Brent Cornelius, a skater from Alaska who won a USHL championship with the Cedar Rapids RoughRiders in 2005. I watched him play and talked to him after games in Cedar Rapids, and the key to recruiting him was that he had become close with a family there. Their daughter was coming to Iowa State, and I said, "This would be a good opportunity to go to school with someone you know. What are you interested in studying?"

"I kind of like computers and anything associated with them," he said.

"You know that the original computer was invented at Iowa State by John Atanasoff, right? They've got a display on campus where you can go see it, and it fills a room. And because you've played junior hockey in Iowa, you've been a resident, so you can get in-state tuition, which is a pretty good break financially."

So, I got him to come and visit, and that was it. The chair of the computer engineering department talked with him, and he was in Ames for four years. On the ice, he was an outstanding player; he was great with the puck and had an amazing shot. He was outstanding, yet very coachable. He played in the World University Games and three straight ACHA All-Star games. Brent eventually played minor league hockey in the ECHL before moving on to use his degree at IBM.

During Brent's junior year, I was closing in on a milestone that carried a lot of meaning for me. Ron Mason had a really positive influence on my style of coaching: power play, penalty killing, faceoffs, everything. He had been an outstanding player, won an NAIA National Championship with Lake Superior State and then an NCAA Championship at Michigan State. Ron was a good friend over the years, and when he retired in 2002, his 924 wins were a college record. I told people at that time that it was a number that might never be passed.

In the middle of the 2007–8 season, Iowa State earned its 900th win since I had become head coach, and the number was up to 912 when that season ended. The next year was my fortieth in Ames since first arriving for graduate school in 1969. Word spread, and the countdown was on. There was a chance to break the record at home during a two-game weekend against Arizona State in early November. Friday was a record-tying night, and on Saturday, we swept the series with a 3–2 victory. After the game, the team presented me with a jersey on the ice. It had my name and "925" where they player number would be. It was a special, memorable night, made all the better because we were at the Ames/ISU Ice Arena with so many people who had been part of getting the program there. By luck or coincidence, I was very fortunate that so many of my milestone wins—the big numbers that ended in "00"—happened at home, and they became occasions for the players and fans to celebrate Iowa State hockey together.

13

BOBBY KNIGHT AND A VOTE OF CONFIDENCE

Iowa State's 2009–10 team was experienced and deep. Brent Cornelius was one of a half-dozen important seniors, and he played big minutes on defense. Brian Spring was a senior and our highest-scoring player from the year before. He had grown up in Iowa and played high school hockey for the Des Moines Oak Leafs, where he was coached by Iowa State alum Doug Borud. Mike Lebler was a junior. He was born in Austria while his father was having an outstanding professional career, and Mike eventually went on to play for the same Austrian team after he graduated. In goal, Erik Hudson had become a Cyclone midway through the 2007–8 season, coming from the British Columbia Hockey League. He was a workhorse in the crease and a big part of our success during his years in Ames. Erik later became the first goalie from Iowa State to play in the World University Games.

That was one of my teams that really played to their potential, probably as well as any team I've coached. We hosted the CSCHL Tournament but lost to Ohio in our second game. Ohio had also beaten us a couple of times in Athens earlier in February. As a result, Iowa State went into the ACHA National Tournament at 27–11–4 with the fifth seed.

The games were played west of Chicago, hosted by Robert Morris. It was a sixteen-team, single-elimination bracket played over five days. Cody Steele from Calgary had a big moment in our first game, getting us past Kent State with a shorthanded overtime goal. Still, it was a costly 7–6 win. Brody Toigo had proven to be a very good scoring defenseman during his first two seasons with our team. He was checked and literally flipped over on his back,

After more than one thousand wins and during more than forty years of coaching, I loved the intensity of game night behind the bench. *Bernie English.*

landing on his neck. Brody was hurt but didn't show it; he actually cracked one or two vertebrae, as we found out later. He kept playing the rest of the tournament but wasn't quite himself.

The next night, we won another close game, upsetting Illinois in overtime with a goal from Derek Kohles. Like Brian Spring, Derek and Brad Krueger had grown up in central Iowa and then gone on to play junior hockey before coming to Iowa State. Now, they had helped us get into the semifinals and one more game against Ohio. We got the win against them when we really needed it, coming back with four goals in the third period. Brad and Brian each scored, and Mike Lebler had two goals for a 4–2 win.

In that tournament format, if you lost a game, you were done. We packed the bus and moved out of the hotel each day. Then each night, we came back, and I said to the person at the desk, "I told you we might be back."

The championship game was against Lindenwood, a college near St. Louis. They had only been in the ACHA for a few years, but we had seen them a lot. Immediately, Lindenwood had six or eight solid players from junior hockey, so that helped them become very good very quickly. Aside from our on-ice rivalry (both of us being in the CSCHL), there was a rivalry off the ice. We recruited many of the same players, and it got pretty competitive. Some of the other coaches used to joke, "Why did you go to

Lindenwood? Well, it didn't cost anything. My dad has a farm, so he donated a load of grain and a cow." Their tuition was lower, and I certainly lost a few recruits to them.

In 2010, Lindenwood was the defending national champion and had started the new season with twenty-four straight wins, including two against us. They won the CSCHL tournament in Ames, and they had convincing wins during their first three ACHA tournament games. Their style was pretty defensive, and we just couldn't break through. Near the end of the first period, an Iowa State player was given a major penalty, and their bench didn't like whatever he had done. It got pretty heated after that. Derek Schaub, Lindenwood's head coach, and I had a couple of shouting matches between periods, and people were thinking, "Hey, they're going to come to blows." We didn't, but it was a pretty major argument.

Lindenwood finally scored in the second period and then scored another goal a couple of minutes later. We couldn't convert any power plays to get back in the game. At one point, one of our players broke his stick and didn't drop it. He kept the lower part and was trying to hit the puck out of the zone with it. That's a penalty, and it put us shorthanded at an unfortunate moment, so it was just a very frustrating night. We lost 2–0. It was a pretty quiet bus ride home, and it was the last time I would coach a team playing for a national championship.

At the highest levels of junior hockey, players have been getting younger and choosing their colleges earlier. For a long time, the USHL and other leagues had been filled with players who had finished high school. They were nineteen or twenty and didn't have a good scholarship offer. Today, a lot of junior players are sixteen and seventeen and have been recruited by NCAA Division I programs before they ever get to the USHL. Many teams in that league stopped allowing non-varsity coaches to talk to their players. I would see it firsthand in their buildings. In places like Cedar Rapids, Waterloo and Des Moines, they made an exception for me.

"You do the right stuff, Al," they'd tell me.

A junior coach might say, "Here's a guy that's on the bubble. Do you have engineering at Iowa State? He's interested in engineering."

When a lot of ACHA teams were looking elsewhere, I still had something to offer, especially for the players who were good students. I emphasized with all our players that it was an absolute must for them to focus on academics. "You can get into school in a few days, but you can get out of here just as fast, so you better not even think about skipping class. Get your assignments in on time, and you better let your professors know which Fridays we are going on the road and when you are going to miss class."

I could also still use deep, long-standing connections for recruiting. The Dubuque Fighting Saints were flying in Grant Standbrook every couple of weeks as an advisor. He would call and say, "Al, I'm going to be in Dubuque. You better get over here and see some players." So, I went over; usually, when I go into a rink, I want the coach to know I'm there but to still be out of sight a little bit. Jim Montgomery was the coach in Dubuque then and saw me slip into the third row of seats with my notebook. He yelled, "Murdoch, get down here. Standbrook is here. Come sit on the bench during practice."

That was how Joe Bueltel came to Iowa State from Dubuque's 2011 USHL championship team. I remember the next fall he said, "Coach, I need to miss a game on Saturday night. I hate to do it, but we're getting our rings."

"Rings?"

"Yeah, we won the national championship last year. We're being presented with the rings on the ice in Dubuque."

Joe Bueltel was a tough kid from Colorado and would settle down rugged teams like Minot State when they came to play us.

Bringing players to Iowa State and being part of Cyclone hockey was still exciting. I wasn't feeling old; in fact, I felt like I could suit up to play. At the same time, the years were creeping by. Our one thousandth win since I became head coach came in February 2011. In 2012, USA Hockey recognized me as the Adult Member of the Year for what I had done at the university, with the ACHA, and for my service as a director. That was also the year I was diagnosed with testicular cancer. I was getting sick and not getting better, and that's how I found out. You don't expect to go in and get that kind of bad news, but it turned out to be good news because I was able to be treated. There's a great doctor here, Dr. Dyche, and he said, "We can take care of that, and you'll be as good as new."

I remember coming out of the operating room on a cart, and I said, "How'd things go?"

"Great. You'll be fine."

Sure enough, I did get better. I missed practice and games for a week, and then I was back, but I couldn't do quite as much and was probably a little more reserved than I had been. It also slowed me down away from the rink.

I used to love running. They have a "midnight madness" race every summer in Ames. The last time I ran in it, I got halfway through those three or four miles and felt like I was starting to lose consciousness. I haven't been able to run very well since, and I miss running. After more than sixty years, I just couldn't run without running hard, giving it everything, but at this point, that means facing the danger of passing out and risking serious injury. I do still play golf, however, and can still find a thrill with that. In 2022, I had my first hole in one.

I had started as Iowa State's hockey coach in the middle of a season, and my time as coach ended in the middle of a season. It was November 2013, and we were practicing at the Ames/ISU Ice Arena. I was going through the routine: individual skills, team skills, power play, penalty killing. I had the whiteboard out, and off in the corner, there were a few players who were not coming over. Instead, they were huddled up talking to an adult member of our program. After I was done with the other players, I went over to that person and said, "When I call the guys over, don't take them aside for something else."

This individual didn't take that very well, so we met one on one after practice, and I said, "You have to understand there's a head coach. When the head coach says something, that's what has to go."

Well, he took his chair, flipped it over in the office and said, "This is bullshit. I'm out of here."

He collected his gear and walked out of the building, and I didn't expect to see him again.

A couple weeks later, just before Thanksgiving, we were playing two home games against Minot State. They were defending national champions, and they were very good again that fall. I'm not sure if they had lost a game at that point. I felt that our team was very coachable. Our goalie Matt Cooper was good, our defense was solid and the forwards were taking advantage of opportunities. On Friday, we won 2–1, and on Saturday, we had a really solid night, winning 4–1 to complete the sweep. That made us 16–3–1 up to that point in the season.

On Monday, I had a message to stop into the business and finance office. I thought Warren Madden wanted to congratulate me on beating the defending national champion and number one team in the country. Instead, he asked a question that surprised me. "You're a Bobby Knight kind of coach, aren't you?"

I don't agree with some of the things the former Indiana basketball coach said. I don't advocate tossing chairs across a basketball court. But when it comes to getting the most out of players—more than they themselves believe they can give—I think Bobby Knight was one of the best, and I admire those characteristics quite a bit. I took it as a compliment. So, I said, "Yeah, we both coach to win, and Iowa State hockey had a couple of good wins this weekend."

I don't know what story Warren Madden had been told about the incident from a few weeks earlier. I don't know his source; I don't know how the version he heard might have differed from what really happened. None of that really matters now. Warren Madden apparently did not admire Bobby Knight and thought of him in the category of things that were wrong with college sports.

"In this day and age," he said, "We have to be careful how we push people. You're going to retire today."

The decision had been made.

It's important to remember that I was not an NCAA coach with a $250,000 guaranteed contract. I was a professor in the Iowa State kinesiology department. Fighting this decision would have meant jeopardizing my job at the university. I wasn't ready to do that, and I wasn't ready to put the hockey program at risk with an ugly public confrontation.

During hockey season, the campus television station had a weekly *Al Murdoch Show* on Tuesday nights. That's where I made the announcement the next day. I said that I wanted to go out on top after sweeping Minot State. I wanted to spend more time with my family. I noted that I had some health troubles in the preceding years. The *Iowa State Daily* and *Ames Tribune* tried to get me to give more details, but I refused to say anything negative about the administration or why things happened the way they did. My wife, Jane, was pretty upset, and in many ways, those were the worst days of my life.

At the same time, I know I'm probably the luckiest guy in the world. As I look around my office today, I'm reminded that people thought enough of me and what I was doing to put a piece of white tape around a hockey puck and mark it with "Win #700, "Win #800," "Win #1,000." I helped build something that touched thousands of lives and wouldn't have existed without me. I was lucky to spend time with Ron Mason and Herb Brooks and Bob Johnson. They all passed away too early, but they each thought enough of me to stop wherever they were at and say, "Al, good to see you buddy." I had great players and assistant coaches and support staff, and I have been fortunate to remain a part of their lives, even though many of them are far from Ames today. And I really have had the opportunity to spend more time with Jane, my kids, and my grandkids. The coaching about life that naturally comes with being a grandfather is the most satisfying coaching I've ever done, and it's given me the chance to share the things I learned from my dad so many years ago.

A more amicable retirement from Iowa State came in May 2021, over fifty-one years after I first came to campus as a graduate student on an assistantship. During my last years as part of the faculty, I taught classes in sports management, golf, and, of course, skating. I had been teaching skating almost since the beginning, and I always did it in a way that was unorthodox.

I would tell the students, "OK, everybody, put your index finger up in the air. You got to wind up the music." And I would make a spinning motion over my head.

The students would say, "What the hell is he doing now?"

I would insist, "Everybody, wind it up." And that was the cue for the girl in the main office to start the music over the speakers—Huey Lewis or Rod Stewart or whoever was recording great tunes that were recognizable and had rhythm.

"Wind it up. This will make you a better skater, because you'll feel the music in your skating."

I got the students to laugh and smile. That's part of what made it all worth doing in the first place, plus it's easier to learn something when a teacher makes it memorable by having fun.

Even after full retirement, I still get to spend some time around campus. Each June, the Ames/ISU Ice Arena hosts a USA Hockey U14 camp for the six states in the Central District. I help administer the camp, and one of my responsibilities is acting as the liaison to Iowa State, as we use some of the on-campus facilities: the residence halls, food service, those type of amenities. Not long ago, I was in a meeting about residence hall room assignments, sorting out the details with a couple of ladies on the ISU staff. The door to their office was open, and a young woman was walking by in the hallway with a stack of files. She stopped, turned back and stepped in. "Oh, Dr. Murdoch," she said, "Your class was my favorite class in four years at Iowa State. I just graduated last weekend, and that was my number one favorite class." The other two ladies I was meeting with looked a little surprised. Their expressions suggested, "You know, this is just a hockey guy you're talking to?" The young woman went on, "You made it so enjoyable. I'd never skated in my life, and I'm not even sure why I signed up in the beginning, but it turned out to be so much fun, and every time I hear Rod Stewart sing "Rhythm of My Heart," I'll think of being on ice skates."

When she left, one of the two women in the office said, "Goodness gracious, that's a vote of confidence."

I said, "Hey, I never wanted to do anything unless I have fun with it."

That type of feedback from a student is something any teacher can appreciate. It is affirming to know you've made an impact. Once you've been a teacher or coach, it's always a part of who you are. I was reminded of that when I went to one of my grandson's youth hockey games not long ago.

Nat Little, who played for me at Iowa State and during the World University Games, has two boys and was coaching their eight-and-under team. At the new rink in Des Moines, I was sitting near the locker room, minding my own business. Nat asked me to step in as the team was getting ready for their game. "OK, we have a special pregame speaker today. Coach Murdoch is going to talk to you about hockey."

He caught me off guard a little bit but not for long.

"Make sure you listen to your coach," I told them. "Make sure you leave it all on the ice. And above all else, when you go home, make sure you make your bed and wash the dishes for your mother. I'll be checking to make sure you're doing this stuff."

It's great to have occasional opportunities like that. Better still, it's great to hear the things I said for so many years now being passed on to another generation. From my kids to my grandkids. From my former players who are coaching—Nat Little, Bill Ward, Jesse Monell, Glenn Detulleo, my son Andrew, and many others—to their players. The kids might be hearing it for the first time, but for me, it's a reminder of what my dad would tell me when I was the right age to be on an eight-and-under team.

"Where winning is a way of life."

"The bigger they are, the harder they fall."

"You don't run to finish second."

INDEX

ABOUT THE AUTHORS

D r. Alan Murdoch arrived on campus in the fall of 1969 and remained part of the Iowa State community for more than fifty years. In addition to coaching the university's hockey team, he was a fixture in the kinesiology department and was heavily involved in organizing ISU intramurals. Murdoch's hockey teams won more than one thousand games and traveled to meet opponents on three other continents. Nicknamed "Doctor Hockey," Murdoch was the first president of the American Collegiate Hockey Association and also the first coach to lead an ACHA team representing the United States to the World University Games.

T im Harwood is a broadcaster and writer based in northeast Iowa. He has been the play-by-play broadcaster for the Waterloo Black Hawks of the United States Hockey League since 2005. More recently, he has simultaneously been the host of a morning news program on KXEL-AM. His previous writing projects have explored Waterloo's rich hockey history, as well as the city's brief stint in the National Basketball Association after World War II.